THE DAYS OF THE SERVANT BOY

LIAM O'DONNELL

First published in 1997 by
Mercier Press
PO Box 5, 5 French Church Street, Cork
16 Hume Street Dublin 2
Trade enquiries to CMD Distribution
55A Spruce Avenue Stillorgan Industrial
Park Blackrock County Dublin

© Liam O'Donnell 1997

ISBN 1 85635 165 3

10 9 8 7 6 5 4 3

A CIP record for this title is available
from the British Library

Cover photograph from the Father
Browne Collection courtesy of the Irish
Picture Library
Cover design by Penhouse Design
Set by Richard Parfrey
Printed in Ireland by ColourBooks,
Baldoyle Industrial Estate, Dublin 13

Dedicated to my wife Kathleen

CONTENTS

CONTENTS

Introduction

INTRODUCTION

This is the story of the days of my youth, in which I saw quite a lot of hardship, living rough-and-tumble as one of a family of twelve, seven girls and five boys.

I was born on 18 June 1923 of hardworking farm stock. Fourteen of us sat down to two tables in a medium-sized kitchen. We had enough to eat and nothing to spend and were scantily clad. We lived three miles from the village of Milford in County Cork. We mingled with all sorts of people, and among those were the servant boys, of whom there were many in our locality. They came from far and near, from Limerick, Clare, Tipperary, Kerry and Waterford, to work – or should I say slave – for the better off farmers, and used their paltry wages to help their own families who were often living in desperate conditions. Poorly clad but very well-mannered, they played hurling and football with us on the local teams, and went to dances known as the fourpenny hop. The big farmers thought little of the servant boys but among my kind they were always welcome. I expect that many of their sons and daughters and grandchildren are now giving an excellent account of themselves in all the countries of the world. In this book I relive the days of the servant boys – and servant girls too – who endured harsh treatment but who were the salt of the earth.

1

The Hiring Fair

This is a day of great importance both to the farmer and to the servant boy, as it is the time when the future twelve months' work is determined. The usual hiring day where I came from was at Charleville at the fair on 10 January.

The fair usually commenced at five o'clock in the morning when a very large gathering of cattle was assembled along the main street of the town. Pigs would arrive around seven to eight o'clock in horse, pony and donkey creels. Business would be very brisk, and buying and selling and clapping of hands would continue all day long. Then around ten o'clock came the arrival of the servant boys and girls and they would gather at the corner of Smith's Lane where it entered the main street. There they would await the arrival of their future boss for the hiring.

It was easy to identify them as they would usually arrive with bicycles, although an odd one would come on foot. Any belongings they had would be tied in a bundle and slung over the handlebars or on the carrier if they had one. The bundles were never too tidy and usually tied up with a piece of rope or a lump of woolly bag twine; a pair of strong nail boots (and a pair of shoes if they were lucky enough to have them) would be exposed and attached to the bike. The boys themselves were a mixed lot, some just left school, others in their twenties and thirties and some middle-aged men, who had clearly seen a lot of hardship.

They were noticeably tidy and clean-shaven for that day to make a good impression. They wore common clean striped shirts, neck open, displaying good hairy chests, which was an indication of strength and a help when hiring. These were the points the farmers looked for and it was known at times for some of them to pull up a trouser leg to see if they had hairy legs as this was also a show of strength. At times if you were watching this you would not know whether it was a man or a horse they were looking for; nevertheless the servant boy grinned and bore all this humiliation. There was no other choice.

The majority of the servant boys smoked fags as they called them, usually the famous old Woodbine, better known that time as 'coffin nails'. Today they are supposed to be poison and bad for the health but they never seemed to do any of them any harm or stunted their growth, as they were supposed to. You would have the occasional older man smoking the pipe or dúidín, as they called it, and quite a few of them chewed tobacco. This they would tell you was to economise as their money was scarce. No matches were required, a small piece of tobacco would do the day and a ounce could pull them through the week. At four old pence the ounce it was a good buy. Men who chewed tobacco were recorded at that time to be dangerous, not that they were different from those that smoked the fags, but that if you happened to vex one of them there was a terrible danger of getting a tobacco spit in the eye. This was indeed a very sore thing and they were capable of giving a direct hit.

I remember one time when one of those men came from a neighbouring farm looking for help for threshing. We kept a few sheepdogs – one rather daring. The dog charged the man who was chewing. He just stood his ground and when the opportunity came he hit the dog with a jet right in the eye. The screams of the dog were unmerciful and he wasn't seen for two days after.

When the moment of hiring arrived prospective employers would be gathered in their dozens, having arrived from the adjoining counties. They usually walked up and down the street a bit of a distance from the boys and girls, viewing their future servants, studying their walk and appearance. Some of those farmers were very good judges. An approach would be made, questions asked: 'What's your age? Where were you working last year? What wages did you get? What size was the farm? What was the name of the farmer you were with? Did you leave on good terms?' – and so on. The present hirer might have some idea of where he worked and judge from that.

Then the examining of hands would commence; they were very well vetted to see if they were good and rough – an advantage. Then the coat would have to come off to see if they had good hairy arms and muscles would be well handled. Some of the boys had ones as big as goose eggs. Then there was the big question: 'Are you a good milker?' This was the most important task. In general at that time a good servant boy would be required to hand-milk on average twenty cows morning and evening during the milking period from March to October.

The time required for milking was two hours – approximately ten cows per hour, and they would be good heavy milking cows. There were also occasions when he would have to milk more than the required amount, if any of the other farm hands were absent or busy out in the fields at hay or corn. The usual pattern about the country was of big, extensive farmers owning from fifty to a hundred cows with from three to five hand-milkers. Milking in itself was a skill; the usual method was damp milking and this was done by pulling the teats of the cow into the hand. On occasions you could dip your hand into the bucket of milk – not very hygienic but that was the rule in those days and the wetting of the hand was like oil to an engine. There was also dry milking which was milking without wetting the hands and some farmers opted for this. So it was the six-mark question when hiring: 'Can you dry-milk?' And quite a few of the boys were well able for this.

Then, of course, there were the servant girls of whom quite a few were employed by farmers. These proved to be excellent hand-milkers; as a matter of fact they were far ahead of the boys and were very good finishers, which meant a lot in milking terms. Some of the more extensive farmers hired girls who were well able for outside work feeding pigs and calves but also working in the fields. After milking the farmer, or the boss as he was called, would go round feeling the udders to make sure they were milked out.

At the hiring fair, when the boy or girl was selected

the next big question was the wages for the year, the term being from January to Christmas Eve. The parties would be asked what wages they were expecting and you can be assured that the discussion took some time. The usual run at that time was £18 per year for young boys, say sixteen years old, and older lads could command around £35, with exceptional cases of £50, all according to ability and appearance. Girls got far less wages.

While all this was going on another factor to be considered was the question of board and lodgings. The hirer would say, 'We keep a good house and table,' indicating that the food would be good, then out of the blue would come: 'Are you good with horses? Can you plough and mow?' This was important as in the usual run most farms did big amounts of tillage. There could be up to fifty acres with wheat, oats, barley, turnips, mangolds – which were the staple of winter feeding – and also a few acres of potatoes and maybe sugar beet as a cash crop.

When the bargaining was about to be completed between the hirer and the servant boy there was much handclapping and holding of arms; the farmer would put his hand tight on the shoulder of the boy to try to convince him everything was OK. All this coaxing would have been about the difference of a pound or two and maybe it would be fought out to the last ten shillings. Should there still be a disagreement there might be a cute farmer watching closely and if the boy in question was a likely looking lad he would be giving him winks and nods to try to get inside his neighbour for a few extra pounds. There was a fair amount of rivalry between farmers who did not like each other and indeed there were many of them in those days. There would be intense excitement trying to encourage the servant boy over to one side or another and indeed this often resulted in a good old fist-fight.

After the long-drawn-out battle of hiring, the boss would usually take his new prize in for a drink – not an overdose, just a medium Guinness (half a pint) or two. Oh how the farmer would boast if he was after taking a boy from one of his arch enemies! No whiskey was offered as that was too dear. I knew of one such boy who was taken for a drink and, as he had never been a drinker, when the boss asked him what he'd have he said he'd have a small Player (ten cigarettes) which was the same price as the medium. They may have been little educated but they were wise.

With all completed the servant boy would cycle his bike, if he had one, while the farmer preceded him in his horse and trap (or maybe in his horse and common cart) to his future destination. It was indeed great enjoyment for a farmer to be homeward bound with his new prize cycling behind him. Should he have done well at the fair he would have had a few extra drinks – maybe a little spirits which was like fuel to fire. He would develop a very loud tone of voice, giving a running commentary to his new catch on the location; he could be heard for miles around and should he pass another pub he'd make a stop for more drink. Now his heart would be getting soft and he'd maybe have taken a liking to the servant boy and while in the pub he'd put his hand in his pocket and take out a shilling or two and give it to the boy. He'd never hand it to him inside – he'd throw it on the ground and say, 'Good boy! Pick that up for yourself!' and needless to say the poor chap would be delighted.

As the farmer usually walked the cattle to the fairs in those days the wife would follow with the horse and trap. She was usually a timid little woman with very little to say about the affairs of the farm. The man usually dominated the household and the fair day was the only chance the woman had of venturing out to town to do some shopping. That day all the groceries were purchased. As they'd say, it was her day off for the messages – tea, sugar, a bit of confectionery, which was a great luxury, the large (7lb) pot of jam – and a few loaves of bread.

These last were also a luxury as the woman had her own home-baking done every day. Sometimes on his way home from the fair the boss would attack one of these loaves and eat the half of it. He was a hungry man fasting since early morning and there was no such thing in those times as going into an eating-house (as they called it). Especially with the farmers all that sort of thing was a waste of money. They'd rather buy a bun or two which would cost a halfpenny each and eat them with a pint of porter. And by God they ate them!

2

The Arrival at the Destination

On arrival at his future place of employment the servant
boy would be introduced to any other staff or members
of the family who were at hand. There was no such thing
as shaking hands; only: 'This is our new man,' a nod of
the head and that was it. In the meantime the boss would
say to the wife who might still be in the trap gathering
her belongings, 'Get down off your perch and get on with
the tay!'

The boss and the servant boy would unharness the
horse and see that he was rubbed down with a brush or
a sop of hay and then well fed and stabled for the night
before they would attend to themselves. Then to the
kitchen and the governor himself would demand to see
what the missus, as he'd call her, had purchased that day,
because no matter what he spent on drink, she would
have to account for every penny. More times than many
he would growl at her when he'd hear the price of things
especially the *sóannaí* [luxuries], as he called them,
meaning the confectionery and jam and the rest. He'd say,
'What the hell do we want them things for; 'tis far from

them you were reared!' In spite of all this he would eat the most of them himself.

There is a story told by a new servant boy who was present one evening when the shindy arose between husband and wife. She was a quiet woman but got high at him giving out to her about spending money. She could stick it no longer and said, 'You are giving me hell about spending money on groceries and I saw you in the pub this evening throwing money on the ground to the servant boy; of course, your hole was open to the new man...' Over she made for the tongs by the fire and the boy made his escape immediately. He did not want to get involved in a family brawl. Indeed it was well known that many's the poor farmer's wife never got a chance of doing the shopping. She only wrote out the list of what she wanted and himself did the job.

When the tay was made after the return from the fair the new man was introduced to his first meal, well treated the first time to show good example, probably a pair of blue duck-eggs, plenty of homemade bread and butter. Bacon could be on the menu, as all farmers in those times killed their own pigs. The usual practice was that the servant boy ate by himself in the kitchen while the boss and herself and family ate in the parlour, a special room away from the kitchen.

I was a regular visitor to those places during threshing and harvest times. Whereas the owners ate well in the parlour the poor servant boy had to do with seconds. On the other hand these poor creatures came from very humble homes and they were delighted to get their bellies full and ate all that was put in front of them. They'd always finish what milk was left in the jug and throw back a fistful of sugar from the bowl. Once they had eaten enough there was no time for relaxation and it was straight away down to business. There was always a lot of work to be done that evening considering that the boss was out all day. Cattle, pigs and horses had to be attended to. Since it was wintertime and dark coming in early the old storm lantern was used to help feel the way around. It was no great light but it did the trick.

Sleeping quarters for the boy were no great deal either. Maybe it was the settle bed in the kitchen, which in those times was as big as a ballroom. This contraption was a kind of floating press which opened up at night and served as a bed. It was folded up in the morning and then it served as a kind of table-cum-press where buckets of water and bags of flour, and maybe horse harnesses, were kept during the day. When opened at night it was approximately six feet by four laid out on the floor with surrounding sides two feet high, mattress, blankets and pillow all enclosed. Indeed it was a hard lie-down.

The mattress usually consisted of two large sacks sown together, known as bran bags. They in turn were filled with oaten or barley straw well packed. It was an important task at threshing time that sheaves of corn from the centre of the stacks were selected for dry straw to use in the filling of the mattress. Not only did the servants use them but they served as mattresses for other members of the families of less well-off farmers. Indeed I slept on one for years as a young boy. When you'd be tired at night from slogging all day you'd lie down and sleep in any class of a bed.

When the month of May would come these mattresses were taken out and laid on the grass to get a good airing. The straw was teased out and if you were lucky to have some spared away in a loft you could refresh the old mattress. It meant that there was always a tight eye kept for a fine sunny day for this job. On top of the mattress there was another covering to make things a bit more comfortable; this was known as the tick. It consisted of a sack-like cover made from two flour bags sewn together, though the better-off had it made of calico. They were well-washed and bleached before being used for ticking and usually filled with feathers of geese or duck which were plentiful in every farm.

The better-off farms had their ticks filled with duck feathers, better known as 'down'. The goose feathers were a bit rough and occasionally would come through the tick and give you a bit of a pinching. If the servant boy was lucky enough to have a tick at all it would be a very rough-and-ready contraption. It was well known that if the boy was hard to get up in the morning the boss would have his tick removed so that his lie-down would be hard and he'd leave the bed fairly fast. Sheets were a rarity; he might have some kind of cast-off blanket to put under him, a few to put on top of him, with some kind of a quilt on top of the blankets which was also a crude affair.

I knew a servant boy who worked on a large farm and his sleeping quarters were an outside house near the cow byre. Quite a number of working-horses were kept on this farm. They were well looked after and when the work was finished in the evening they had special covers put over them for a few hours. When the boy was going to bed at night he would take one of these covers and put it over him. He did this for the duration of his hire, all unknown to to the farmer, as he would have put the cover back in its normal place before the boss arose.

Many of the boys were very well versed on how to keep warm; one such fellow used to collect old newspapers and put them on top of the mattress, under the tick and between the blankets for heat. Of course according to these boys the old bunks where they used to sleep were a breeding ground for fleas. Flea powder became a part of the bargain like board and lodgings. Otherwise the boys would have been crawling.

As we have seen, in many cases the accommodation would have been an outside shed or a loft. The latter was over the farm kitchen and the entrance was from outside by a crude kind of stairs at the gable-end of the house. The loft was not a very healthy place to live and some-times had no window, the only light coming from an old lamp that required pawing around in the dark. The one advantage was its privacy; the boy could wash and shave there at will whereas if he slept in a settle bed he would have to go out to an outhouse to do the necessary. There was no running water in those days, let alone bathrooms. Water for washing had to be collected from an old barrel filled with rainwater outside at the end of the farmhouse.

Some farms had the blessing of having a pump in the farmyard. Another way of having a constant supply of water was to have a kind of concrete tank built at the end of the haybarn. This tank was usually twelve by six by five feet high and all the rain that fell on the hayshed was diverted into chutes and at the end of it a downpipe brought the supply into the tank. This ensured a regular supply of water which was used for many purposes in the farmyard, washing clothes for the house, cleaning milk churns and buckets and mixing animal feeds. It was used for boiling big pots of spuds for feeding pigs.

Water from the well was used for the kitchen and all human consumption. Each farm had its own supply of spring water which was sited as near as possible to the farmhouse. Sometimes, however, it might lie some distance away and water had to be brought by horse and cart. This was a daily occurrence but if times were busy the women would draw it in buckets. In winter the water was bitterly cold and many a servant boy or girl had to use it for washing. If the woman of the house had a kind heart she might oblige by giving a kettle of boiling water to take the sting out of the cold water.

Having been acquainted with his new living quarters the new boy would begin to get adjusted to his new surroundings. The morning following his arrival he would get a complete briefing from the boss on all the farm animals, the cowhouse and other livestock apartments, and especially the feeding house and boiler where all the food for cattle, pigs and horses was prepared. In the boiler house there was a very large open fireplace which was a blessing to the boy as in very frosty weather the place was nice and warm at night and there was no objection to him sitting there. During the day the fire would be in full swing boiling ten-gallon pots of potatoes for pig-feeding and also boiling water to provide hot drinks for mashing cows, as they called it. The fire came in handy for the boy especially in wet weather. There was no stop for him all day, except for his meals, and at night when the day's work was over his old clothes would be damp, and it was a great place to dry them.

The servant boy often had his bed in these boiler houses or in the loft above, if there was one, and the fire meant that the place was fairly comfortable. Sometimes in winter he did his washing there. The overalls were done once a week to remove the dirt and odour of the farm, so too were the shirt and socks. Many a time I've seen a lump of rope tied from one wall to the other and all the boy's duds, as he'd call them, hanging up to dry. Likewise this was a great place to have a wash or shave when no one was looking. It was well known for the servant boy to bring in a big bath, fill it with water and strip to the skin to have a good swill-down. After that he was off for the night, fresh as a deer coming out of a lake.

3

THE ANIMAL QUARTERS

The serving year began in the heart of winter when all
the cattle were tied in their houses. They had to be fed
morning and evening with hay and roots, maybe turnips
and mangolds, which had to be prepared by a hand-
operated pulper, a crude kind of a contraption. Some dry
stock had to be looked after, and pigs and horses. The
cowhouse was the most important centre of the servant
boy's work, especially in winter; he spent almost all his
time there. This building was not far from the house and
one end of it opened out into what was called the pound
field. This was between three and five acres in size and
it was here that the cows stayed during the day after
morning feeding until they returned in the evening to rest
for the night. This field, in some places called the stand,
was in continuous use from November to the end of April.
It was fairly well ploughed up with anything from forty
to a hundred cows threshing around in it all day. Any dry
stock would be out-wintered in a suitable field away from
the farmyard.

The cowhouse could be a very large building with

single or double ties. A double shed was big enough to hold forty or fifty cows each side, tail to tail, as the expression was, with either a hipped or round roof of galvanised or sheet iron. The field entrance was wide enough for a horse and cart to get in, about eight feet wide. There was usually a similar opening at the other end and both were fitted with iron gates covered with sheet iron. The cows were tied up side by side with a tying space of three and a half feet, in timber stalls. These consisted of two eight-by-four-inch beams stretching from one end of the cowhouse to the other at top and bottom. Uprights, one fixed, the other movable, were attached to the beams. The movable one was attached to the lower beam by a bolt which allowed it to move freely back and forward. When it was opened it allowed the cow to put her head through to get hay or any other feeding that was in her compartment. When the head was through the stall was closed and held by a simple hook.

The animals were quite happy there with great ease and the freedom to move their heads any way they wished; and they could lie down in comfort. The cow had a feeding space at her head of about two feet and there was a wall three and a half feet high running the whole length of the cowhouse to separate the feeding passage, which was four feet wide. Hay was brought there during the day from the hayshed which was attached to the building. This system was the same on both sides of the house and since there were haysheds on both sides it was an easy matter to load the feeding passages with the required amount of hay for the beasts morning and evening. This hay was all loose; in those days there were no bales. Turnips and other roots were delivered from the feeding passages in a similar way. There were openings at the ends of the passages through which a barrow full of roots could be wheeled. These doors opened on to the farmyard pits where turnips, mangolds and potatoes were stored. These were grown extensively on most farms and there could be up to a hundred tons of these crops stored in the farmyard. On the very large farms they had long sheds for storing this cattle feed; otherwise it was kept in large pits or mounds about sixty or seventy feet in length and six or seven feet high rising to a ridge at the top. They were well covered, first with a little hay, and then layers of straw, oaten or barley, were made into a kind of thatch, finished off with rushes which had been cut and drawn from some distance away. To finish off, the pit was covered with sods of clay to keep out the winter frost and rain. No matter how bad the winter these stores were as dry as powder inside where the roots were.

There was no water laid on to the cowhouse and drinking bowls were never heard of in those days in rural Ireland. All pound fields had either a running stream or pond of water where the animals could get their drink; that was why they were let out during the day. The old folk believed, too, in letting the stock out for exercise. It helped them to be more active after lying all night on concrete. Unlike the present day there were very few animals suffering from stiff joints or sore legs. As some of the boys used to say the only stiff legs and sore joints were those suffered by the men who worked with the cattle and they got it not from lying on concrete but from hard old beds, bad boots and damp clothes.

The cleaning-out of cowhouses was done with the aid of a horse-drawn butt that was brought into the cowhouse at one end and had the manure forked into it as the horse moved slowly along. When the butt was full the stuff was taken and piled somewhere on the farm; the butt had a lever which when pulled dropped the contents. The heap was usually close to a field that would be sown with roots the following spring. This made it easy to spread and indeed it was used as fertiliser for pastures as well. So after the required number of journeys the cowhouse was completely cleaned out. For obvious reasons the single cowhouse was not as convenient as the double. In many cases the smaller types were cleaned out using a wheel-barrow and the manure brought to a dungheap often close to the house. These heaps were long and wide since they had to hold six or seven months' manure but they were kept very tidy until the spring when the cows were put out to grass.

4

DOWN TO THE GRINDSTONE

Having been introduced to his new environment and got the feel of his duties about the farm the pattern of the serving boy's life was soon established. He would rise at seven o'clock in the dark of a winter morning. The woman of the house would also rise early and if they were well-off and had a servant girl she would rise earliest of all. The boss would also rise early on the first few mornings until the boy got into the hang of the work.

The fire was kindled to the light of oil lamps and the first tea of the day was made. On the previous night some of the firewood would have been quenched with water and left for the following morning when it was assembled on the open hearth. Fireballs of old newspaper soaked in paraffin oil were put under these sticks, a match was put to them and there was soon a good fire. In some cases turf was used: a few sods were assembled round the fire at night and these would be good and red in the morning. Some farmers would bring in a fist of good dry hay and use that instead of paper for a good blaze.

With the fire in full swing the big metal kettle hanging

on a crane would be lowered down by pens and crooks and it would not be long until it started to sing, indicating that the water was on the point of boiling. It did not take long: you must remember that this kettle full of water was hanging over the fire all night and would be fairly warm to start with. If the boss was rising to help he'd usually shout from his room, 'How's the kettle going?' and back would come the answer from the kitchen, 'She's singing!'

The big teapot was then produced – a good-sized enamel one – and a few fists of tea from a big jar were put into it. This jar was called the tea canister and would hold a few pounds of tea; the teapot would hold about six pints of tea. Then the tongs would be produced from beside the hearth and some red cinders would be raked out to the side of the fire. The teapot would be placed on this so as, they'd say, to give the tea a good pull and have it good and strong. The old folk used to say, 'Fair-haired tea is no good.' You'd want it good and strong, so good, they said, that you 'could trot a mouse on it'. They also used to say that a house with brown-stained mugs was great for a cup of tea and that tea was also good for the lining of the stomach. They believed that if the stomach was well lined from strong tea sickness was unable to enter, and especially so in wintertime. Indeed I knew some of these farmhouses I visited and they'd have the teapot by the fire all day. When you entered the kitchen the kettle would be singing over the fire and they would add a sup of water to the teapot and introduce you to a good cup of tea. This was great for the men on the farm who would return to the kitchen whenever they felt like a good cup. Indeed the women did not leave it go with them either; they too were always fond of a good cup of tea.

Another quaint old custom was that at the fall of evening some one of the family would collect a *gabháil* (armful) of kippins (*cipíní*). These were small bits of sticks that would have fallen from the trees round the house and they would be dumped in the corner near the fire so they would be good and dry for the morning. These with an armful of hay or papers would also produce a good blaze. I remember many mornings when you would be out early and you would get the smell of the burning hay. This was the case especially on calm frosty mornings and the smoke could be seen for miles billowing from the chimney. At that time farmers would make it a matter of pride to try to be the first in the locality to send up smoke. This was so it could be said of them in conversation, 'I see you were up early this morning.' There was the occasional man who did not rise too early and he would not light the fire until late. Some neighbour or other might say, 'By God, you don't get up too early. I didn't notice smoke until late in the day.'

'Ah,' he'd say, 'but I wet the tea before I went to bed and it was grand and warm and well drawn when I got up.' He would continue, 'Remember I keep a good fire and it stays smouldering all night.'

So he'd keep them guessing and not make them any the wiser.

After the tea was finished in the morning the servant boy, fully clad in working-clothes, overalls and strong boots, would make a quick exit to the cowhouse, accompanied by the boss on the first morning to introduce him to his future duties. The first job was to give the cows their hay from the feeding passage. This was done by the light of a storm lantern, as, remember, it was a dark winter's morning. There was always a good supply of hay available – and it was good hay too. In those old days it had to be well saved and it was fed *ad lib*. When that was done the boy would go to the back of the cows and remove the dung from under their legs and move it back to the channel or passage. This he swept vigorously with a coarse brush. When that was done it would be time for the roots to be fed to the cows, usually, as I have said, turnips or mangolds.

The big wheelbarrow would be brought to the root-crop pit beside which the pulper was located. The barrow was usually a homemade contraption capable of holding a few hundredweight [100kg]. The roots were put into the pulper and cut into what were known as finger slices convenient for the animal's intake. The boss would stand at the end of the pit and with a hayfork (or two-pronged pike, as it was called) he would feed the turnips and mangolds into the pulper, releasing them as he drew back the pike and letting them fall on to the knives of the slicer. The servant boy would, of course, get the hard end of the job; it was up to him to work the handle that turned the blades.

The pulper was wide at the top and narrowed to a cone shape at the bottom as the roots fell down. If they were not slicing properly the boy would use a big lump of a stick to press on them to get them on to the knives and hurry the job. Indeed sometimes he might use his hand to apply pressure, a very dangerous venture, and many the man nearly lost a finger at it. Another trick for making the roots slice was to split them in halves before you'd feed them in.

The pulper stood on four legs which were in a sloped onward position for holding purposes. It also had four short handles midway on hinges so that it could be moved from place to place by two men. The handles were let hang while the machine was working. Under the pulper was a big square board or sheet of iron on which the roots dropped, and when there were sufficient slices on this the barrow was filled from it by means of an implement called a navy shovel. Then the boy would proceed to the feeding passage. When you'd look at this big barrow full of roots you'd wonder if it wasn't a horse rather a man that should be used for pulling it. It goes to show us that there were great strong men in those times and I often think it was no wonder these farmers examined the boy's legs and hands on the day of hiring.

The barrow having been pushed to the feeding passage, the roots were then fed to the cows. Each would get a few shovelfuls and on top of this a few fistfuls of barley meal which was carried in large buckets known as five-galloners. Barley was widely used as it was a great belief that cows near calving required it. There were several other rations fed such as parta and beet pulp – a must in every big farm. Sugar beet was grown extensively as a cash crop and when delivered to the factory entitled the seller to his quantity of pulp, which was a very cheap feed. This came in dry form and was steeped in barrels overnight. During the Second World War when tobacco was scarce many's the hard-working man smoked it – and what a smoke!

In the springtime when the cows started calving, bran was widely used as this was the farmer's friend. When the cow had calved a kettle was boiled and poured over a few handfuls of bran, let cool and given to the cow. If there was a sick animal bran was the means to cure her. The old trick with bran was if the animal was constipated to give her a good hot drink of bran and if she was loose or scouring to give her dry bran. Both cures worked. The old folk would tell you bran was better than any vet or doctor for man or beast. I have seen poultices of hot bran applied to swollen joints on men, and if they happened to have a boil on their neck or any other part of their body the hot bran was applied there too. Indeed boils were a regular occurrence that time, whether caused by rich food or not enough food.

With the feeding of the cows finished the next item on the programme was the calves. These were housed for the winter in sheds approximately eleven by twelve feet and there could be up to twelve of them in these sheds running loose. Against one wall would be a hayrack and on the opposite wall a big timber trough. Hay would be put into the rack and roots into the trough, mixed with a dash of meal. The barrow with the roots was left outside the door and the feed was taken in the big buckets to the calves' trough. It was a rough job because these calves were fairly strong and contrary when it came to feeding. In those days, too, dehorning was not heard of and you could imagine these calves with four- or five-inch horns bucking loose in a house and you trying to get through with a bucket full of roots. I can assure you you'd want all your wits and strength.

One boy who worked for a contrary farmer used tell us how the boss accompanied him around for a few mornings at the feeding. One morning as he was going in through the calves one of them upended the bucket and spilled the pulped roots. He just turned around and gave the old calf a bit of a kick. His back was turned to the governor and before he knew what had happened he got an almighty kick on the arse. He turned around mad and the boss pointed his finger at him and said, 'Every time I see you kicking a dumb animal I'll give you the father and mother of a kick on the arse.' So that taught the poor chap a lesson and as he said, 'If I ever got vexed after with the animals I made sure the old boss was fields away before I'd do anything.' And indeed many's the poor servant boy got a severe gruelling from these horned calves for they'd hit you with their head and give an upward swing. Anything the horns would stick in, they would bring it with them and indeed they left many's a boy without an arse in his trousers.

Next came the pigs. Every farmer kept five or six sows and sometimes more, and some of these sows would have bonhams with them. There would also be perhaps thirty or forty pigs fattening for market. Sows were first to be attended; they'd be let out from the bonhams and fed by themselves in the open yard. The food consisted usually of boiled potatoes mixed with barley meal. This feed was already prepared in half-barrels in the boiler house. The potatoes boiled earlier in the morning or the day before were waste or culls from the main crop. Sometimes Indian or yellow meal was mixed with these and as always the dash of bran was thrown in to keep the stomach right. If the bonhams were big enough they'd also get a little feed and the fattening pigs were fed on the same mixture. There would be maybe fifteen to twenty of these fellows in a big loose house and it was no joke to make your way through these fellows to the feeding trough with two big buckets of food for like the calves they could be rough, ignorant gentlemen. Their troughs were in divisions of about ten inches in sets of about ten yards long with divisions of timber to keep them in their separate places. Otherwise there would be food all over the floor. Circular troughs made of cast-iron were also used, good and heavy so as to keep them from being tossed about. These had iron rails dividing each feeding section.

Of course all these pigs had to be controlled in their environment and this was done by putting rings on their noses. Each pig would have five or six rings. Without them they'd have their house in a quare old state. The sows would have a share on them also as they'd have the whole place ploughed otherwise. Ringing pigs was a special technique. The animal was held by the two ears and a looped rope at the end of a three-foot stick was put into the animal's mouth; the stick was twisted until the rope tightened on the snout. Then it was no problem to implant as many rings as you wished with a special pliers. The animal couldn't move but I can assure you there would be some screaming.

When ringing sows it was a different set-up: there was a special narrow pen into which the beast was driven and the door was closed. It sounds cruel but it was like hooking fish. You had to play around until you got the mouth open and the rope in. Then you had to tighten the rope by twisting, and hold her steady, keeping your hands out of her grasp, because she'd be contrary and watching to get a hold of the operator with her teeth, which were deadly fangs if they caught you. Many's the man got a bad bite from a sow. It wasn't so much a bite they'd give you as a tear for if they got hold of you they'd just squeeze and drag. Ringing pigs was a kind of profession of its own and I was a capital hand at it in my youth.

The bull who was the mainstay of every farm also had a ring on the nose. It was an easy thing to ring this fellow; just get his head through a cattle crush or gate. The ring was an open swirl with a point on one end and you just pressed it home through the nose and a little screw joined it together. Some of the old people had different ideas: they used to redden a poker with a point in the fire and stick it through the nose first and then apply the rings. They used say you had better control of him when using a staff to lead him out. This staff had a six-foot handle with a spring clipped on the end and this did control him well. The bull was a very dangerous animal and all servant boys got the strong advice: 'Don't ever turn your back on that fellow.' That indeed was a true saying for many men were killed by one of them because they were careless or trusted the beast. But the bull was one animal you could not trust. Even at feeding time the bull had to have a separate house with half-doors top and bottom. The top one was opened first and the boy would catch the length of chain which for convenience had been left dangling when the ring was put in. This would usually be about two or three feet long and it could be caught by the workman and held tight from the outside whilst the staff was put on the nose and then he could be tied in the house to a hook on the wall whilst his food was put in for him.

When the bull was let out with the cows the chain would be increased to about seven or eight feet. This kept him controlled a little although when he got used to the long chain he was well able to control it. When walking he'd keep the head sideways so as not to stamp on it, because if he did, it gave the nose a severe chuck which quickly brought him to his senses. No stranger ever dared to go into a field where a bull roamed with the cows. If you were taking a shortcut through the fields you'd always size up the herd of cattle to see if there was a gentleman amongst them and it was a usual occurrence for some farmers to have notices placed on the fence saying 'Beware of the bull' and indeed many's the farmer who had no bull running with the cows would have notices of this kind so as to keep out intruders.

Bull owners would keep the animal enclosed in a paddock by the farmhouse; the idea of this was to keep the bull from being used by small farmers, say those who had only about ten cows, as it would be too expensive for them to have a bull for servicing. Their usual device was if they had a cow rambling, or as they honestly called it, bulling, well then they'd go to where there was a bull with cows of a neighbouring farmer and taking their cows with a rope tied to their horns they would work their way into the field by gates or, if necessary, by making a hole in the fence, and so get the job done. Of course this was all done under complete cover of darkness whilst the owner slept soundly. There were some very wise small farmers who'd have a rambling cow. They would keep her tied up in the cowhouse during the day and at the dead hours of night they'd release her and drive her towards where there was a bull. She'd make her way to him without any trouble and arrive back again, job complete, and the bull would always return to his herd.

Next on the feeding line were the horses, maybe four or five or more all according to the size of the farm. There usually would be a good-sized pony for the handy work around the farm and for the trap car on Sunday. Horses were very easy animals to handle – no fuss with feeding. You could walk in freely to them, put the hay on the rack over their head and oats into a feeding trough in the corners. A few mangolds were also given, which they liked very much.

Having completed all the feeding the servant boy would return to the dairy, which was beside the cowhouse, and there he'd wash his hands and dry them with a cloth which was provided for the job. This could be a piece of calico or the remnants of a flour bag well washed. He'd then go to the cowhouse with bucket and three-legged stool to milk a cow or two kept during the winter to provide milk for the house. These cows milked during winter were known as strippers, ones that were not in calf and which provided just a few pints of milk. These cows were sold off when the flush of milk started to come in spring from the calved cows. When the strippers were done the milk would be strained into a special bucket used for the farm kitchen purposes. The straining was done with a nice clean piece of muslin cloth which was looked after by the woman of the house who washed and scalded it with boiling water after each milking. It was then put out to dry on the hedge until the next milking. When all this was done, the boy would clean his boots with the yard brush and return to the kitchen with the boss, bringing the milk with him for the main breakfast.

Before talking about the breakfast I have to tell the story of a servant boy from an adjacent county who was very new to the district. He'd been to England for many years and had also been out in foreign countries as he had joined the British army and of course had seen many sights which our Irish country folk had never heard of. So on his first morning, which was in the winter and frosty, after having finished his first feeding with the help of the boss he was told: 'You now have to milk the stripper.' The new buck had never heard that applied to cows and he turned to the boss and says 'O, Jasus, have ye one of them here too?' and the boss not knowing anything better says, 'Of course we have, man, and I couldn't do without her.'

'Well let me tell you,' says the boy. 'I've seen strippers in many countries and many a climate but never on a frosty morning. Isn't it rather cruel to make a poor woman naked on a morning like this!'

5

BREAKFAST

All morning jobs completed, the new servant boy now arrives in the farm kitchen for a well-earned breakfast. The eating habits in those times were quite different from today. The term 'servant boy' finished in the 1940s when the more suitable name of farm labourer or farmhand was introduced and the majority of farm workers from then on lived in what were called tied cottages or farmhouses. These belonged to the farmer and these working men lived with their families and went home to their meals.

Now for the oldtime servant boy sitting down to breakfast at the master's table: he'd probably be eating on his own in the kitchen, while the boss and his family ate, as I have said, as the parlour. This was very well furnished, sophisticated and comfortable, with food far in excess of what the boy would be getting. Should there be a servant girl employed she'd be eating with the boy. The kitchen table would normally live up to what the boss had promised at hiring; it would be laden with homemade brown bread and butter, which was never scarce as this was purchased at the creamery in fifty-pound boxes. A good chunk of it was always on the table. Eggs were also on the menu. So after a hard morning's work the servants would usually dive into a good hearty country meal.

The usual fare was a pair of big blue duck-eggs. These were in abundance in all farms as flocks of ducks and hens were kept, and with good feeding and warm fowl houses they laid eggs continuously during winter. Bacon could also be available for breakfast. It was the country custom to boil a big chunk of home-cured bacon, say eight to ten pounds, in a big ten-gallon pot. It did for the dinner and supper and there was always a quantity left over for the following morning's breakfast. This was good bacon as every farmer killed his own pigs and they'd usually make the ones for their own killing good and fat. You were sure of a heavy cut, as the old folks would say. You'd want a depth of four to five inches of fat on the back and there was no discarding of it. The servant boy would relish this seeing that he had spent up to three weeks at home with his humble family where he'd seen little meat since he left his last employment on Christmas Eve, when his hiring agreement terminated. Now that he had a good chance, as they'd say, of throwing his legs under another man's table, he'd make good use of that.

The duck-eggs would be boiled in a good big black saucepan on the open fire and more times than many they arrived on the table as hard as bullets. As the boys used say, 'You could play football with them,' and this is where the butter came in. A good lump would be put in when the top was removed and mixed up and down with plenty of salt and I can assure you they were relished.

Cheese would also be on the ready as this too was

bought at the creamery in large cakes of up to twenty-eight pounds which were really delicious. Like the butter, cheese was made in abundance at the local creamery and all suppliers of milk got it at a special price so there was no scarcity. You could eat your fill. Tea which had been made in a big black enamel pot would be sizzling on red coals by the open fire and left there until it was well drawn and was good and strong. The servant boy if he was on his own would have to attend to himself and this indeed was a great advantage; there was nobody looking down his throat. And he could also provide himself with some little refreshments for when he'd finish work that night. As he got used to his surroundings, he'd help himself to a grain of tea out of the canister, a little sugar, a lump of cheese, some butter – whichever was most convenient, and nobody to see what he was doing. They say there was no one the wiser while the boss and his family were away in the parlour. As mustard was widely used the boy would always be on the lookout for the empty mustard canister, as it was called. Mustard came in dry form and the disposed-of container was very convenient to hide in the coat or trouser pocket with the grain of tea and sugar. The tea could be made at night in the boiler house for this is where the poor servant boy would retire to when the day's work was done. You must remember he was not wanted in the farmhouse for, God help us, in the eyes of these well-to-do farmers, he was only the servant boy. Having mixed with these lads who were humble and genuine it grieved me that they were treated as if they had some kind of plague. But that was the sad part of life then.

You'll remember the boiler house was where all the cooking was done for the pigs and there would be a great fire there all day and it would still be smouldering at night and was good and warm. The majority of servant boys had an excellent sense of humour and would tell you some great jokes about the dining habits. I remember one boy who worked for a fairly large farmer who was noted for being a miser, when asked what the grub was like said, 'It's like this: he's very generous. The boss will usually say to me, "Go aisy with the bread and butter but you can use plenty of salt."'

There were many very generous farmers who kept good tables and then there were the stingy ones who always tried to pawn over seconds on the servants. We used to hear regular complaints, such as: a certain servant boy and girl used to eat together and the bread provided was very hard so as to make it go further. One day it was rock-hard and cutting it was impossible. The knife kept hopping off it; so he shoved it down the table to the servant girl and said, 'You can ate that,' and she in turn didn't like the look of it and shoved up to him again. He said, 'We kept at that until we wore out the lump of bread on the table.'

While all this was going on the boss and family dined in luxury with toast and maybe a good fry of bacon and eggs, which were always on the ready. The boy filled his belly the best he could at the kitchen table and when he was finished he washed it down with what milk was left in the jug and then he would do his own washing up. It was not a big job as there would just be a big mug, a knife, spoon and maybe a fork, if he had meat. There was no such thing as a side plate and he'd usually leave everything ready for his next meal. He'd give the table a rough wipe down, as was often the case with his cap.

6

CLEANING THE ANIMAL HOUSES

After breakfast the boy would then proceed to the animal houses to clean them out. The first to be attended to would be the horses. The boss would accompany him on his first morning. The manure from the stables would be put outside the door for removing later. The place would get a good sweeping and a fresh bed of straw would be provided and hay put in the mangers. The horses would then get a bit of a quick grooming and rub down, maybe with a brush or sometimes a lump of hay. A halter was then put on the animal and it was brought out to water. When it had its fill drunk it was returned to the stable.

Next in line for feeding were the pigs, the animals of perfume, as the boys would refer to them, and for the feeding of these the servant boy would don a bag apron to keep his overalls clean as there would be terrible excitement when he entered their quarters and you had to keep the buckets of food rather high in case of a spill for these were rather stubborn gentlemen. The manure that came from the pigs was rather on the soft side and this had to be brushed out through a hole in the wall on to a slope so as to flow away from the pig house into a pile which was drawn away at a later date. The house had to be well cleaned and old bedding removed through the door as this contained straw which would not flow through the hole. Then a fresh bundle of straw was brought in from the hayshed for bedding down the animals.

By the time this was done there was a quare smell from the boy and his overalls. At times the boy and the girl did not see eye to eye and in that case the boy would take off the bag apron which would be covered with pig dung, bring it into the kitchen and put it up on the crane over the fire so as to annoy the girl. When it got the heat the aroma was desperate and this caused quite a stir. The girl wouldn't be too civil making the tea that evening. But 'twas enjoyable and they got over it. The boss and the missus enjoyed this crack and they'd talk about the good sport their servant boy was. Although the pig is held to be a smelly and a dirty animal yet he has his own house manner. When the pigs are bedded down in one corner of the house they'll keep this part clean and they'll use another part of the house to manure and urinate and *never* on their bed.

The sows with bonhams that were fed outside their houses in the open yard in the morning and left to roam around the open space had now to be collected and returned to their living quarters. These damsels were a contrary lot; we often heard the saying 'as ignorant as a pig' and these were that, and stubborn as well. Sometimes they refused to go to their houses and the cure for this was for the boy to go to where their offspring were, catch one of the bonhams by the ear and lift him up. When this was done he'd give an almighty squeal which could be heard quite a long distance away, the mother would immediately come at a fast canter, growling with vexation, and when she got near her quarter the boy would drop the youngster and run for his life, leaving the door open for her to enter. His escape was necessary for if she got hold of him, he wouldn't forget it in a hurry. Sows are very contrary when nursing their piglets and though there might be ten or twelve sows out together they'll always recognise the squeal of their own.

The boy when settling into his duties was always in the boss's eyes for the first few mornings but when he'd show good signs of improvement he was completely on his own. A very important task was getting used to the dog or dogs as every farmer had one or two of these animals and they were part and parcel of the farm. Since these animals had had a different servant boy the previous year the present man had to get these dogs accustomed to his ways and sometimes he could be rejected. He depended on them while he was working on their premises so he had his work cut out for himself trying to be friendly with them. For a start he chatted friendly to them and would bring a bit of meat or some nice morsel from the boss's table to help him coax them. After some days they'd usually accept him but only after giving him a lot of dirty looks and growls. In the end they'd settle down as they'd have no other choice.

Having completed the feeding and cleaning of the pigs, the boy's next task was cleaning out the cowhouse. This was a job for the horse and butt or tumbling cart as it was sometimes called. This butt was a modern type of cart which was easily unloaded by pulling a simple lever at the front. The complete load slid off and when the horse moved forward the butt tipped up to its natural place for transport. Now with the horse harnessed to the butt cart the servant boy proceeded to the cowhouse and starting from the bottom gate he'd move through the centre of the cowhouse as this passage was sufficiently wide to accommodate the cart. The cow manure was then forked into the butt. The horses had more sense than some of the boys or the farmer, for as you were cleaning the house you just called the horse by his name and said, 'Up a little!' and the horse would respond perfectly for the next amount of manure to be put into the butt. In those times every horse on the farm had his own name and responded to it. I've seen four or five horses in a field answer if you called Paddy, Molly or Bill or whatever the name and come to the call. Indeed in the cowhouse the horse was fully capable of manœuvring this journey on its own. The manure was then dumped for later spreading.

If required for root crops or potatoes the dung was usually dumped in the corner of the field in a large heap, so it could be near the crops and well rotten in the spring when the drills were made. With the cowhouse cleaned there might be four to five loads of manure. The boy then moved to the calf houses, reversing the horse and butt to the door, of which the upper half would open leaving the bottom closed. The dung was then thrown out over the half-door on to the cart and again transported out to the field and put on the dung pile. The calves would then be bedded down with bundles of dry straw to keep them nice and warm.

The pig manure was not taken to the field immediately as it was considered a bit too soft. Instead it was let season and dry on a heap outside the door until the spring, when it too was used for root crops, especially carrots as it had little straw through it. (At that time quite a lot of carrots was grown for horses.) Pig dung was also used for the cabbages, an acre or two of which was usually grown for winter feeding to cows. This cabbage was known as flat Dutch, which was a very large cabbage and well able to stand up to winter frost.

With the house cleaned the cows were let out to the pound field to get a bit of exercise and have a drink of water. They were usually let out about 12 o'clock and returned again about 3 or 4 o'clock all according to the weather. While they were out of the cowhouse this gave a chance to the servant boy to finish the cleaning of the house, to put the hay in the mangers and give them a good bedding of straw. The feeding troughs were also cleaned and the feeding passage adjacent to the hayshed was well packed with hay. Some of this hay would be given to the cows again at night, about 8 o'clock. The oldtime farmers would say that this kept the animals very contented at night and indeed this was very true.

Now that the tidying up was done, bags of spuds, or as they were known then, praties, were brought in from the outside pit to the boiler house, thrown out on the floor and small ones and damaged ones were selected for boiling for the pigs and the sound potatoes kept for human consumption. Nearly all the animals would get some of these potatoes, including the hens, ducks, turkeys and geese which were to be found on every farm. These potatoes when selected were put into a big half-barrel of water and with the handle of a fork or shovel they were bounced up and down to remove the dirt from them. This was done by hand. The boy would remove his coat and with sleeves tressed up he put his hands into the barrel of potatoes with fingers held together to make sure the dirty water drained off them. Then they'd be transferred to the ten-gallon pot which was hanging from a big crane over the fire in the boiler house. The crane was sometimes known as the fire gate as it worked on the same principle. It could be moved out from the fire to be loaded with the pot and swung in again over the blaze.

Some of these pots were capable of holding a hundred-weight [50 kg] of potatoes. They had three strong legs for resting on the floor. Incidentally the washing system of potatoes for animal feed being thumped up and down with handle of shovel or stick was also applied to potatoes for human consumption. There was no brushing or fancy washing in those days. The servant girl or woman of the house would fill the big bucket at the pit, go to the water barrel at the end of the haybarn and give them a good thumping and then go to the kitchen and put them into the pot for the dinner.

Now the potatoes in the boiler house would take many hours to cook, usually running late into the dark of the night, and it was the servant boy's job to keep fuelling the fire with plenty of timber which was always available. No coal was used as this was a luxury confined to the farmhouse; at the price of £2/10 per ton it was considered too dear. The boy would usually do other jobs around the farmyard, returning occasionally to keep an eye on the pot, and when the time was right and the potatoes were boiled a shovel would be applied to the spuds and they were well mashed until they formed a good gruelly paste ready for mixing with meal for feeding. During this process the servant boy would usually pick out a half-dozen or so, maybe with a bit of butter from his pocket, which he'd be after helping himself to whilst at the supper, and have a damn good feed. He might have too a mug of milk which he'd have fetched the same way as the butter. Of course all these things were done whilst the occupants of the house weren't looking; the milk was always readily available in the dairy, which was convenient to the cowhouse. The servant boy had the freedom of all these places as he had to check the animals from time to time and always before he'd go to bed.

7

ALL IN THE DAY'S WORK

When the majority of morning jobs were finished it would be coming up to dinnertime which usually was after 12 pm. A whistle or loud call would summon all servants to their grub. This was given by the man or woman of the house. The man would usually give a loud whistle but the woman would put the two hands around the mouth to form a kind of funnel and with all the pressure from the lungs a loud call would be given such as 'Yoha!' in a drowning fashion and this could be heard from a long distance. If it happened that the workmen were far out the fields in the farm the caller would usually climb up a ladder at the end of the hayshed and that would help to deliver the message.

The servant boy would usually make a stop at the dairy coming to the dinner and give the hands a wash and dry. Then the boots got a rub of the yard brush and maybe a ball of hay would also clean them. He was now ready to take his place at the table in the kitchen.

Praties, plate, knife and fork were put on the table by the woman of the house or servant girl if they had one.

Also an enamel jug of milk and plenty of salt. The kitchen table where the boy ate was just a plain common lump of a table and the potatoes were thrown loose on this. His plate would also be enamel and the same plate saw many a servant come and go. When new this was of a white colour but now it would be chipped and dis-coloured; some of the boys would call it the leopard plate there were so many spots on it. Meat was served on this plate, a good chunk of pig's meat as they were always killed a-plenty on the farm. Fresh meat such as beef or lamb was never seen by the servants but of course the householders would have this as a luxury at weekends

Turnips and cabbage were the staple vegetables. They were also plentiful and the juice of the turnip and cabbage was very much relished. The boy would usually drink a few mugs of this as it was reckoned that this was great for the health and served as a good medicine for the bowels. In some farmers' houses new milk might not be available so usually skim or buttermilk was supplied to the boy. The bacon served would always be very fatty but fat or not he'd eat plenty of meat, praties and turnips and cabbage. There were no side plates; he'd just peel off the skins on the table. Many's the servant boy or girl never used their knives or forks. They just peeled the praties with their fingernails. You must remember that the majority of these lads and lassies came from poor large families where knives and forks were a luxury.

I, in my time, have seen many of these at the local threshings peeling praties and eating meat and vegetables with their fingers. If they tried to use a fork and knife they felt very awkward. When the dinner was eaten the boy would make a sup of tea as he'd have the use of all the supplies for same in his dining quarters and he'd have, as they say, a good wash down. Homemade bread was also available.

When all this was finished he'd prepare a feed for the dogs, who were always admitted to the servants' quarters and let hang around the servants' table. Praties leftovers, skins and all, the vegetables and juice and any bits of fat meat were all mixed on the boy's plate with a dash of milk and put on the floor. The dogs wouldn't be long cleaning this and indeed, God help them, I often heard the boys say they'd have no trouble washing the old plate, the dogs licked it so clean. Then after that the boy might throw them a cut of bread dipped in the juice and this was also relished by the dog. This was sometimes known as the binding between dog and man as a dog always had an affection for the person who filled his belly.

The boy would usually tidy up his table, just a quick lick to any utensils he was using, and leave them on the table ready for the next meal.

While all this was going on the boss, the wife and family would be dining in the parlour. They had, as they'd call them, different *sóannaí* from what the servant boy had. Nevertheless Paddy, as we'll call the boy, was happy and contented after filling his belly and drinking a few mugs of strong tay. He would drink plenty as often after a good feed of salty bacon he needed to quench the thirst. Mentioning the strong cup of tea which was always a welcome guest, many of the old folk attributed its strength to the quality of the teapot, for this vessel lying by the fire on the red coals all day would never be empty.

So what tay was left in it would be brewing for hours and the inside of the pot had built up a black hard core like tar which gave the cup the required strength and flavour which was relished by all. This big metal kettle would be lowered until it landed on the red coals. Turf or timber would be added to the fire and it was often said that the smell and taste from the boiling water made the tea very healthy and desirable. When I think back on it a lot of it was true as the old folk who lived simply were very healthy and indeed there were very few doctors required.

Now that the grub was completed and the table left tidy for the next meal it was time to attend to any necessary jobs outside. Usually in wintertime there would be a few hours to spare before the evening's work. There might be timber to cut as there was always plenty of this around the farm. Perhaps there would be a big whitethorn, ash or beech tree to cut. This was a job for the servant boy and there were no chain saws in those times. He used a good big axe and an old-time handsaw and if the timber was fairly large the crosscut was used. These were usually six feet long with timber handles on each end and were required to be worked by two men; usually the boss would help at this sort of work. Cutting timber this way was a very slow process. As was the saying in those times: 'It was a decent type of hard labour', but in spite of all this hardship there was many a big tree felled by this method as there was no other way. When these big trees like ash, oak, beech or sycamore were knocked they had very large trunks and these would be cut in four or five feet lengths and split with a sledge and wedges into good big chunks.

The advantage of the five-foot lengths was that they'd

be going into big kitchen fires, sometimes six feet wide. In the winter when you'd stack up these fires with this type of timber it would be so warm as to put you out of the house, as they used to say. Coal was used only for the parlour fires by the well-to-do and the poor people might buy a ton or two for the Christmas. I remember going to a coal merchant's and getting a good load of coal for £1. Those were the good old times; thing were cheap but money was very scarce.

After the dinner a few hours would bring it up to cow time, when the gate or door at the end to the pound field would be opened and the animals would start strolling in. Although there might be fifty of them they'd all go exactly into their own places as orderly as soldiers lining up for roll-call and Paddy would be inside waiting and proceed to tie them up in their respective places. Of course it wouldn't all be plain sailing: he'd get the odd kick and maybe a little dash of cow manure and an occasional lash across the face from a dirty tail. It was the cow's way of letting him know that they commanded that part of the farmyard. As all cattle in those days had horns they could give him an odd lift of it, and if by chance they got your coat or pants caught it was a definite tear. Anyway they wouldn't catch the flesh, so that was all right with Paddy.

This would bring the proceedings of the day up to 4 o'clock when he was entitled to a cup of tay and a light snack. Then the usual feeding for the evening would start and it was the morning's work all over again. Roots which were already pulped and hay. Oats and hay for the horses, sows and fattening pigs and all of them to be bedded down and fed for the night. If there was a bull in question he'd be brought out to water, given some hay and roots and his bed freshened up.

When all this was completed the boy would bring in some timber and turf to the farmhouse for the night. He would take some to the boiler house as well, for there was always a fire in progress here for boiling pots of potatoes to have them ready for the morning feed.

All this completed, it was well into the dark of the evening and coming up to suppertime. He would return to his usual dining-place in the kitchen where the kettle would be boiling over the open fire and if he was lucky his supper might be ready for him depending on the humour of the woman of the house. All he had to do was wet the tay. He ate alone unless there was a servant girl employed, when she'd join his company. Supper was also fairly good in the majority of the farmers' houses. There was plenty of food – maybe cold bacon if there was any left after the dinner and if that was not available he'd have a pair of blue duck-eggs which he'd boil himself in the black saucepan. Sometimes for speed he'd put the eggs in the boiling water in the kettle. There was plenty of butter and homemade bread. There were, however, places where servants were treated scantily and maybe rationed to one egg. After a time as the boy settled into his job and maybe proved himself to be an excellent worker he'd be getting a few extra shillings and be in a position to buy himself the odd loaf of white bread. This was a great luxury. This was called a pan loaf but not sliced as there was no such thing in those times. And he cut this in thick skelps, as they called it, about two inches thick and he'd toast this at the open fire and with plenty of butter on it he'd relish this.

Now, finished his day's work, he had plenty of time to look after himself at the supper. He was now a king in his own right and they'd be talking about the grand loaf of bread they had as sometimes the homemade bread was not up to standard. A lot of it was made from the farmer's own ground wheat and the woman of the house might bake only once a week when she'd make a good few cakes. After four or five days this bread would be fairly hard and as the boys would say, 'I took the cake out for a while and played football with it; it made it a little soft.'

I knew a servant boy who worked for a fairly prosperous farmer and the wife never baked; she wasn't able. They used say she came from a very well-to-do family and she brought a good fortune into the man she married. This substituted for her not being a good housewife. Anyway he used to tell us they had Christmas every day as it was always white loaf bread and they also got the occasional pot of jam – a complete rarity.

Where a servant girl was employed it fell to her lot to do the baking and hopeless bakers they were. Of course her bread would be eaten only by the servant boy and herself. Little blame to her for God love her sure she had never seen a cake baked in her lifetime at home. One thing for sure the lads would tell you: always have the bread soda available for if not you'd be killed from indigestion. Nevertheless they survived and got on and ate their bellyfull.

8

RELAXATION

Now that the day's work was finished the boy would gather himself out of the kitchen as his company was not wanted by the boss and his wife and family. So he'd go to the boiler house where there were the remains of the fire for pot-boiling. He'd have an oil lamp, maybe an old single wick yoke hanging on the wall by the fire or maybe an old storm lantern. This was also a paraffin-oil lamp which gave poor light. It had an old glass globe which moved up and down and was normally used for moving around the farm at night. That is why it was called the storm lantern. I have been in the company of some of these servant boys trying to shave with these lights and a small bit of broken mirror. They'd strip to the waist and with an enamel pan of water and a good lump of carbolic soap give themselves an excellent shave. Safety razors as we'd call them were just coming into their own that time and the Mac's Smile three-holder blade was very popular.

They were, however, expensive. The safety razor cost about a shilling and sixpence and the blades cost a penny each. With money so scarce you'd need five or six shaves from each blade and the method for getting all the use out of each was by sharpening them. I've seen very shrewd boys doing this by using a wine glass or a jam pot. By holding the blade in the inside of the glass, pressing tightly on the centre as you moved over and back and reversing the blade occasionally, you could put up a good edge.

Having completed shaving the boy could now sit down by the boiler fire and with the light from the lamp darn his socks or sew a tear on his pants or coat. The boys were handy at this sort of work and always there was an old paper or book to read for those who were able.

Quite a number of servant boys had their sleeping quarters outside the farmhouse and this was very much preferred by the boy as he had a good bit of privacy and he could come and go as he wished.

It was indeed rough and tumble but he could keep his bits and pieces nice and private. He could keep his clothes tidy maybe hanging at the end of the bed or on the wall and always he'd have a good sheet of brown paper to cover his best clothes so as to keep the dust off them. Wardrobes were a luxury but he might have some kind of an old press to keep his few possessions and a small table for a late-night snack which he relished at the end of the night.

The outside sleeping quarters might be a loft over the shed, a corn store or boiler house and entrance was by a stairs on the outside or maybe a ladder. These stairs or ladders would always be crude contraptions and it wouldn't do for the lad to be intoxicated or he might have trouble getting up to his bedroom. If a ladder was the means of getting up to bed you'd put this up at night and take it away in the morning. This would give added comfort and privacy. Indeed there were some good jokes between the boys when they'd get acquainted with the locality and meet other lads like themselves. At night they'd meet and maybe visit each other in their sleeping quarters for a chat or a game of cards.

It was a well known fact that these lads were full of tricks and devilment. I knew of one such case where the servant boy had a few lads visiting him one night and when they were leaving they took the ladder with them. Of course the poor lad knew nothing until the next morning and his problem was how to get down. Sometimes there was ten to twelve feet of a drop from the loft door to the ground and the boss couldn't be allowed to know a thing about it for the boy would be allowed no more visitors. This was a strict rule. So when the boy would get caught in a problem like this he'd pull the bed to the door and tie a blanket to one of the legs. This would get him down part of the ways and with him hanging to the blanket the drop was not too bad. The usual thing was to have a length of rope in the bedroom and it was then easy to alight and get your ladder back quickly and nobody was the wiser.

For the first few nights the boy would take things easy; he might not venture out far at a time until he'd get well acquainted with the place and then he'd start to ramble, usually around 8 o'clock in the evening. There was always a village a few miles away where other servant boys rambled to meet their own kind. So friendship would start up. Though there were always a few pubs in the place they were completely out of bounds to the boys as money was very scarce and drink was out of the question.

As the servant boys ventured out to the local village they were warmly greeted by many of the local lads. That is how I met many of them and when I think back on it, it was always a nice score to have a chat with these lads. Although not educated they had wonderful manners and most of them were widely travelled and very entertaining. I am sure they always felt happy to have a chat with some of us locals as you'd sense that they felt the loneliness away from home and their loved ones, and the boys would honestly let you know their homesick feelings.

I'll always recall the way they were on their first visit to the village. They would walk up and down on dark winter nights through the streets which were badly lit. There was no street lighting in those days – only dim reflections from little shops and public houses. The residential houses were dull and dark as windows were always heavily curtained to keep the prowlers from outside looking in.

And for the want of starting a conversation they'd be looking for some place to buy a stamp as some of the little shops used to carry them. (Of course the post office would be shut down for the night.) The boys were always anxious to let them know back home how they were getting on. It was often the case that the boys wouldn't be able to write. If they failed to get that stamp they'd usually find one of the boys who'd be going to the creamery in the morning and give him the penny for the stamp. On their visits to the village at night they'd also be in pursuit of some envelopes and notepaper. These could be expensive at that time so as a substitute for a writing-pad they'd go for the cheap type of school copy as all the small shops carried a good supply of these and also ink and pens which were then required articles for correspondence. Since money was always scarce the boys would usually divide the bottle of ink between them. That saved a bit of pocket money and I often saw boys adding a few drops of water to the ink so as to prolong its use. The copybooks at that time cost twopence or threepence and the ink could be fourpence per bottle for the cheap stuff and sixpence for the good ink. The lads would say there was more gold in the dear one. Ballpoints were not available at the time. All village shops were open late at night and they usually carried a good supply of all these commodities or luxuries, as they'd be called, including a good supply of fags which were very high on the boys' agenda. It was the same with the servant girls. The popular choice was Will's Woodbine, known then as 'coffin nails'. They were sold in packets of five for twopence, also in tens and twenties. Smoking was kept on a light scale during the weekdays but at the weekends they went a little bit heavy when they were out socialising.

There were usually a few smokes got out of each cigarette and it was then put out or 'topped' and put away in a little box. At that time the Oxo [meat cube] box was the ideal article; it was neat and compact and fitted nicely in the pocket. These Oxo boxes were very popular, being made of tin, and the Woodbine packet would fit nicely into them. This box would also protect the butt or topped part of the cigarette.

Matches were also a very important part of the purchase.

You'd get a little packet for a halfpenny. There were twenty to thirty matches in each packet and it fitted neatly into the waistcoat pocket. They too were used sparingly. One economy practised by the boys when they were working out in the field at crops, spreading dung or other chores, was a good sod of lighted turf in an old can or bucket with holes on the side of it and that would stay red all day. When the boy wanted a smoke he'd take out the sod of turf and give it a gentle little puff. It would redden up and when he'd lit the old fag he'd put the sod of turf back in the can or bucket until the next smoke.

When the servant boy went to the local village to buy a few necessities he'd be usually on the lookout to meet new friends and join company. He'd look for boys like himself who were working in the same district. They'd make the homeward track together, usually stay out late chatting and getting accustomed to their surroundings. There were no time limits set for them to be back to their beds. I often spent time with these lads as quite a few of them worked in our locality. They were very interesting and entertaining, some of them having travelled widely to many of the surrounding counties and brought stories and crack with them. Quite a few of them were talented musicians, well able to handle the tin whistle, melodeon and concertina.

Some could play the fiddle which they would have carried with them and as we'd say in the south you were sure of a *gealtaigh* [lively] night sitting on the fence in the dark on the side of the road listening to them. Sometimes they'd bring their music to the village and a little congregation would gather around. During the playing you'd find them breaking into a jig or a reel and one or two of them would take to the road and dance to their hearts' content. Before long you would have a large congregation all enjoying the crack, and the ones who were able to sing would break into a rousing song which could be heard for miles. Mind you they never created trouble and were never a nuisance. They always had great thought for children who might be going to bed or old people who didn't like noise. When they'd be breaking up at night a few of them would accompany each other and maybe end up in one of the boys' sleeping quarters. The old mouth organ or tin whistle would be produced and more entertainment provided. Of course we must remember that the majority of the lads slept away from the main dwelling so they'd always be out of harm's way. Then while the dying embers were in the boiler house fire a cup of tea was made and with the last drag of the Woodbine they'd thoroughly enjoy it.

Before he'd go to his bed the servant boy would light the storm lantern and check that all stock especially cows, horses and pigs were OK. As often happened during the checking of cows there might be one near calving and if that was the case he might have to stay up the night. If it was a big dairy herd, calving would start in January. If this happened during the boy's rounds he'd draw a sup of milk from a cow who was already giving milk as this was needed to make more tea while he was looking out for the sick cow. Most nights he'd have smuggled out tea, bread, sugar and butter to have a little snack for himself. He might have a few good praties put aside out of the pig's pot earlier in the day and these would be put by the fire on the red coals and left there to get a bit of a roasting. They'd be very nice and tasty with a bit of butter and salt and a good mug of milk, and as the boys would say a bit of a snack like that would help you to have a good night's sleep.

Remember that there was no need for these hard-working men to watch their weight or diet for they worked more than twelve hours a day for six days a week and approximately six to eight hours on a Sunday with no day off. When we consider today's farm labourer with his forty- to fifty-five-hour week we can't help compare the men of the '20s, '30s and '40s who worked up to eighty hours a week and indeed in those days it *was* work.

I remember myself when I started working on farms in the late '40s the first breakthrough was the half-day on Saturday. Some of the old men were reluctant to take their half-day in case they'd lose their job as they lived in the past in the old tough days. And although the half-day came into force they still had to work on a Sunday. The men who had this relief were outdoor men with their own little houses. The man or boy who was living in with the farmer had to forfeit this half-day and many of the old-time gentlemen-farmers did not accept this regulation. I heard some of them saying, 'I'd rather sell out my cattle and farm than give the servant boy a half-day.' It took a good number of years to get this law to be properly enforced.

Getting back to the '30s, when the boy was finished at night, before he'd go to bed he'd put any old damp clothes he'd have after the wet day around the fire in the boiler room on the back of a chair. His socks would be put on the crane to get a good drying, for Wellington boots were not heard of in those times. It was usually the hobnail boots or, as they were called at the time, the strong boot. As with everything there were good and bad ones. The good ones were dear ones and the boy usually went for the ones that suited his pocket, the cheap ones. With continuous wear around the farm the socks were bound to be damp as cheap boots were not capable of keeping out the wet. The boys would always remove the socks after their supper and put on a fresh pair for roving at night. It meant that the working ones would be fairly dry for the following day. Next morning when they removed them from the fire crane they rubbed them well between their hands so as to freshen them up a bit.

When going roving at night they sometimes put on their Sunday shoes or 'low' shoes, as they were called, so as to look a bit decent. The collar and tie were never put on on a weeknight unless the lad had a date. Otherwise all was reserved for the Sunday night's dancing.

Some weeknights the boy would stay in to do some work for himself, washing a shirt or few pairs of socks. He'd do his washing in the boiler house. This was an understanding with the boss and part of his bargain. He'd be provided with soap, a washing board and a large basin which was a galvanised contraption with two handles, stood about fourteen inches high and held about ten gallons of water. This was placed on the back of the chair with the old-type washing-board standing in it. The board might be of timber or galvanised with ridges on it and with the bar of carbolic soap the shirts and socks would be scrubbed up and down on it until a good lather of suds was produced. Then with the help of hot water from the large pot over the fire the duds were well washed. These were then rinsed in a mixture of hot and cold water and well squeezed with the hand. They were put out to dry on a makeshift line, probably in the hayshed or another outhouse. Should the weather be fine they might be put out on a hedge or bush and left there to dry. When they were brought into the boiler house for airing they'd be hung up on a line of twine. Before the bath of suds was thrown out the boy would usually take off the boots and socks and give the feet a good washing to refresh himself. Afterwards he'd feel fit and spruce and ready for anything.

Collars for shirts, which were a separate piece of clothing, were given special attention at washing and kept in a clean environment when they were ironed while damp and had a bit of starch applied. These lads were fairly handy at these jobs. The woman of the house might supply the iron or the boy might even have his own equipment. This iron was an old triangular box with shutters at the back. The heater as it was called was separate and also triangular. This was solid iron and would be put in the big fire in the boiler room and left there until it was red. From here then with the help of the tongs it was put into the box and the shutter at the back closed. Then there was a shield which fitted neatly over the box. This was of a silvery nature which gave a smooth performance. The boys had a trick of their own for testing: they would hold the iron on a sloping position and spit on it. If the spit hopped off it was ready and safe for ironing and wouldn't damage the article. The ironing was done on an old table with a piece of cloth over it, usually made from flourbags. They'd iron and starch these collars damp, placing a piece of damp cloth over them, and the final result would be an excellent shirt collar. This was important as the girls in those times would always be judging these lads by their nice laundered collars.

All these odds-and-ends jobs would keep the boy occupied at night and should he be finished early he'd turn to darning socks. The servant boy was a dab hand at this, too, whether the hole was large or small.

9

SOCIAL LIFE

Many kinds of entertainment were available when the day's work was done. On the winter weeknights it was just meeting some of their friends and maybe getting acquainted with some of the working-class people who were living in the area. They soon got friendly with those living in cottages, of which there were many. The residents of these houses had sons and daughters like the travelling or journeyman servants out in service with farmers far and near and they had quite a lot in common with each other. If any of the family were working locally they were bound to give a call at night to the old homestead as there was a great loyalty amongst the poor working-class; the families were indeed very close. When visitors arrived the pack of cards would be produced and it wasn't money they were playing for as it was not available. They'd use matches as a substitute for the pennies. I knew of one house where the woman kept loose buttons in a jar on the mantelpiece and she'd dish out a fist full of them to each cardplayer. They'd have a roaring night and indeed they'd fight over a button as if it were a pound note.

These were never serious; it always ended in great fun and it was quare times when you'd see a grown man playing with matchsticks or buttons. A far cry from the big poker games of today. There was a bit of gambling for real money in those times by the well-to-do. I recall a servant boy coming to a house one night and announcing he had learned a new game called poker. All listened attentively and the man of the house said, 'You can't play that here as we have only one poker and she never leaves it out of her hand all night, poking the old fire.' That was the end of the game of poker.

When the cards were ended all would gather around the spark of a fire and chat for a while telling stories. They were mostly all lies, for they were great at them. One old man in particular would always say when he'd visit a house, 'Have ye any news? I don't care what kind it is; lies or anything like that will do me.' After a while of chat the cup of tea would be introduced as kindness was always amongst the poor, humble and all as they were, and indeed the cup was always welcome.

Card drives were a regular thing in the wintertime. The sessions were called 'gambles' and each working-class house in the district would have them in their turn. I never missed one myself. We'd travel for miles around the country to them in the winter. As prizes there'd probably be a pair of chickens, ducks or geese or the odd turkey and, in some cases, a pig.

The usual charge was a shilling (five new pence) and these gambles went on until small hours of the morning. The game played was Forty-Five. When the tea was made there was plenty of loaf bread and jam and this, as I've said, was a novelty. There would usually be a big crowd at these functions, eighty to a hundred people all crowded into these cottages, and games would be played in several rooms in the house. (Beds and other furniture were removed from each room.) Eight people would play at each table with good audiences looking on. This went on until the players were eliminated, down to four at the finish.

Now at these gambles there would be a few good musicians amongst the boys and they'd have brought tin whistles, melodeons, accordions with them. The concertina was very popular since it was considered to make sweet music for house dancing. The servant boys would have developed these skills from an early age. Having come from poor backgrounds they'd have little else to amuse themselves at night and from most cottages this music would ring out, accompanied by the sweet sound of the old gramophone which was a must in every house at that time. It was from these instruments they learned their music. The usual make of the old gramophone was His Master's Voice and at all gambling houses it was the in thing to purchase a few new records for the big night. You'd have the very popular 'Cuckoo Waltz', 'The Geese in the Bog' or 'The Siege of Ennis' going at full blast. There would be a boy or girl put in charge of the gramophone and their job would be to keep the needles changed and the gramophone wound up. This had to be done after each record was played. There was a handle on the side of the box for winding and sometimes after a night's playing the needles would be getting blunt and there'd be a blur in the sound. However, there would usually be someone among the crowd who'd be a good hand at sharpening and with a bit of a carborundum stone he'd keep the used needles in top condition. Indeed it was a common practice for someone or other to carry a bit of a stone in his pocket for the job.

As night wore on at these gambles one of the musicians would be called upon to entertain the crowd, whether with fiddle, melodeon or concertina. When they'd start playing they'd never think of finishing. 'Twould be as long as a wet week and then someone would be called to sing a song and like the musicians there would be no ending to this. Nevertheless they were all very enjoyable. In the height of the jollification some party would shout, 'Have you all that song?' and the singer would answer, 'Yes, I have.'

'Well,' they'd say, 'We have had enough!' and that would bring an abrupt end to it. The caller and others would be looking for a change in entertainment.

The stepdancer would be called to oblige. As was always the case the half-door would just be lifted up off the hinges and placed in the middle of the kitchen for the dance, whether it be hornpipe, jig or reel. The idea of the half-door was to give a good sound and bounce to the dancer as all houses had mud floors at that time, especially the poorer houses, and the mud floor was a very dull place to dance on.

Most houses had half-doors then on the principle that although there was a full door going out from the kitchen to the yard there was also the half-door outside that. So in fine weather the full door was opened and the half-door closed to keep wandering animals and poultry out. Pigs, goats and cattle wandered very near to these houses and you had a bit of security when the half-door was closed. However, the donkey who was attached to every cottage or small farm would come and gave a look in over the half-door. He'd maybe linger there for some time and he'd leave his calling-card before he'd go away. It was the same with the hens. I often saw them fly up over the half-door and make their way into the kitchen. They would lay their eggs up in a box by the fire and after that announce their job done by cackling. They quickly made their exit with a little help from the woman of the house.

Anyway the half-door was now serving its purpose for the dancer and, the Lord save us, they'd knock sparks out of the door dancing and always had a good few steps of their own thrown in which were not in the book. 'Puss' music was very popular for the Irish dancing. A boy or girl would take the tissue paper from the silver that was around the cigarette in a packet and place this paper around a hair-comb or rack, as they called it in those times. It was the finest puss music that was ever heard; as they'd say, 'Twould make a man or woman that was crippled jump for joy!' Of course, puss music got its name from the face, which was then often called the puss.

When it was announced that puss music was the order of the night the boy or girl in question would get ready, opening a packet of Woodbines and taking out the silver and gently removing the fine tissue paper. This was put round the comb and given a rub of the tongue and now the puss-musician was in business. All the stepdancers would be up on their hind legs and rearing to go.

As the night wore on the gambling continued. The

losers were eliminated and the survivors would play on at a separate table for money and were not interested in dancing or music. The money in question was one old penny per score of forty-five. In the gambling part it was three games of Forty-Five for the big prize as they called it, the poultry or pig. Before the gambling started the rules were announced by one of the senior folk, loud and clear in a stiff stern voice from a very stern man. 'Keep your hands well above the table in sight of the players while you are dealing the pack and remove the Joker.' The speaker's eyes would wander around and hesitate for a moment on those he'd suspect of cheating.

Some of the boys were very shrewd gamblers and would play in pairs. There would probably be eight at a table, so each winning pair would advance on to meet other pairs. These pairs would work in tokens to their partner which were hard to detect. I learned all of them in my time from being in their company. I often played partners with them and you'd have a rehearsal previous to the play. The tokens would be as follows: a rub on the nose for the five of trumps, which was the best card, a pull of the ear for the knave and the hand touching the chest for the ace of trumps. Some of the old men who were lifetime gamblers would shout at us and say, 'Keep your bleddy hands to yourself or we'll put you outside the door.' You'd think we were playing for a small fortune. Indeed there was many the queer rumpus at the gambles and you'd find a lot of men turning to the opposite side of the road when they'd meet some of these chaps whilst out walking.

The kitchen would be kept for the music and dancing.

There'd usually be some one or two with a concertina, melodeon or fiddle, as they called the violin then, and dancing was of the rough nature with half-sets and barn dances, oldtime waltzes, quicksteps and foxtrots. When the dancing would start the woman of the house would immediately put a chair on its back across the front of the fire in case any one fell into it while the kettles were on full boil and big teapots sizzling on the red coals by the fire. It was the thing at the time to borrow kettles, teacups, cutlery from some of the good neighbours who'd bring them and they coming to the gambles that night. Needless to say all these small houses and cottages were lucky to have even one kettle and teapot and enough cups for their own use. I have been to some of these poor houses where there were big families and have seen these unfortunate creatures drinking tea out of jam pots. At that time, too, the jam pots were made of tough crockery, not like the light glass ones of today. The father or mother would say in a loud voice, 'Put in the milk first in case you burst the jam pot.'

Indeed I have seen jam pots being used at gambles when they'd run short of cups if there was a big crowd there. Tea, loaf bread and jam were on the menu all night and the visiting girls, dressed in their best of fineries, were very busy all night attending to the boys. Of course they'd have their eye on some one of the visiting lads. Around Christmas there would be the barmbrack or the woman of the house if she was handy would have a currant cake baked. This was a great luxury and it might be served to some friends of the family there who'd be brought to one of the rooms and get a little extra treatment unknown to the rest of the gamblers.

The crack would continue until about 5 o'clock in the morning when they started to break up. The man or woman of the house would announce it was time to go home as the cock was crowing. This was a special omen to clear the house, a signal to the morning. In those days you'd have fathers who had brought their daughters to the gamble and trying to collect them was when the real trouble would start. At the breaking-up the boys and girls would start to pair off with some of the servants who would have been throwing eyes and winking at some of them all night. Naturally the fathers would be very angry when the daughters were missing; you'd never seen such a fuss: men running from bedrooms to kitchen and out around the little sheds outside looking for the girls. In the heel of the hunt the girls would emerge from some hidden corner, cool, calm and collected as if nothing had happened. These boys and girls were no children, as they'd say, no greenhorns. The majority of these courting couples would be in their late twenties or early thirties with plenty of sense and the back teeth well up. Some of the fathers would be threatening their daughters using the phrases: 'I know where you were. There's no dust in my eyes and conduct yourself now or I'll complain about that fellow and yourself to the priest.' Behaviour that would not be approved of today.

Some of the lads would appear and ask the father if it was all right to give the daughter a lift home. You'd think it was a taxi they were talking about but sure it was the old iron horse, the bar of the bicycle. Indeed I remember one tidy lad who kept a nice Raleigh bike with a nice kit bag attached to the saddle. He'd keep a nice soft cushion in it to make the sitting more comfortable on the bar of the bike. As he'd say, it was just to make the girl happy. But they would tell you that the bar of the bike was a sore yoke on the arse if you had to travel far.

Still after a hard night's gambling and dancing on a mud floor you'd be damned glad to get your legs off the road at the breaking up of the night. All would be returning now to their own quarters and the boys and girls would about arrive in time to start the day's work and there was no rest for them only, as they say, just get down to the grinding stone. They were rough grinding stones them; some of their bosses were not happy with their boys going to these gambles as they'd say they weren't up to the job the next day and not able to do the same amount of work. But there was nothing they could do about it as it was part of the lifestyle and enjoyment for the servant boy and girl. I heard many the boy say that at the end of the day's work after the night's gambling he'd just roll into his bunk, clothes and all, and sleep soundly until the next morning.

10

THE SUNDAY DANCE

Next and most important in the life of the servant boys and girls was the Sunday night dancing. Unlike today there was no Saturday night dancing, for that night was strictly reserved for the Sunday night's preparation. On Saturday night there'd be the monthly visit to confession, the visit to the village shop to get razor blades and the old packet of fags. If the old money was anyway plentiful the boys would treat themselves to the luxury packet of Players or Gold Flake so that they could cut a dash with the girls. Then they'd meet the other boys and girls and plan for the following night. Dancehalls were aplenty, one in almost every village and town, and you'd have an odd good ballroom out in the middle of nowhere and you'd think nothing of travelling twenty to twenty-five miles to a good dancehall. Of course, the average dancehall in those days was a kind of a glorified cowshed except that you'd have a good timber floor and you could swing to your heart's content as the proprietor had it well dressed with plenty of Lux toilet flakes. They'd do a great job on it. The flakes at the time were used for washing clothes and came in hand to make the dance-floor slippy.

I used to cycle with the boys to all dances, as I said, often up to twenty miles and maybe more. There were no cars and if you got a puncture you might have to walk a quare distance home or cycle the old bike on the rim. And with the roads of bygone days you'd hear the old ramshackle for miles on a quiet night. For there were potholes as big as barrels and sometimes when repairing potholes they used sharp stones and shovels of clay to keep them together. It was not easy to keep tyres right on the bike and with little money you were not able to replace them on the bikes too often. As for repairing a puncture it was a waste of time using solution and patches unless it was on a fine Sunday and you were going to a hurling or football match. Then you might attempt it.

You had to turn the old bike upside down, resting it on saddle and handlebars. With the aid of two old pennies you'd remove the tyre, take out the tube, and using the sandpaper striker on a matchbox you'd clean the tube. Next you applied solution from the tube in your kit to patch and tube and stuck one on the other. Sometimes you would light a match and hold it a little away from the tube and patch as this would help it dry fairly quickly. Replacing tube in tyre you'd pump it and you were again ready for the road. Of course before all this operation you'd have to find where the puncture was. By pumping up the tube when it been completely removed from inside the tyre you could hear the escaping air and with the help of the wet tongue and maybe the odd spit you were bound to find the exact spot. There was another emergency trick which was great when you had to pinpoint the exact spot where the air was coming. You'd then let out what air there was in the tube and holding the spot between your teeth, tie it with a bit of twine and you were in business again. Indeed I often saw lads having no twine use a shoe lace and it would do the job. Of course you then mended the puncture properly at a later date with solution and patches when you had plenty of time.

As for Sunday night dances, there was a great variety. You had the fourpenny hop from 8 pm to 10.30 pm. Then you had what was known as the Cinderella, eight to twelve midnight and finally there was the occasional all-night dance which lasted from 10 until 5 in the morning. These were occasionally held during the wintertime and believe it or not they did dance all night long at them. The admission to these all-night dances was a half a crown (two shillings and sixpence), and supper was served during the night for one shilling: plenty of bread, butter and jam and for an extra sixpence meat, maybe a bit of ham.

Now the fourpenny hop was great old crack as the boys and girls were there in their finery, dressed to kill, as they'd say. They all would mix at the dance, servant boys, girls and the fairly well-off. Class distinction was kind of forgotten then. In the summertime it was grand but it was a bit harsh in the winter. But hail, rain or snow they all made out for the dances. In those days, too, a girl could travel all the lonely roads on her own and be quite safe. No such thing as rape. They were all highly respected.

The boys usually wore the strong boots when they were going to the dance with the low shoes tied to the carrier of the bike. About a half mile from the dancehall they'd remove the boots and put on the low shoes, having kept them nice and clean and dry. The hobnail boots would then be rolled up in a pile of sacks they'd have with them and these would be hid in the ditch in a marked spot and left there until returning as it was dangerous to tie them to the bike. All the bikes were stacked at the back of the dancehall or there might be a house convenient to the hall where they'd be left in the backyard. The owner, probably an old man, would take care of them for the big fee of a penny. Every bike carried a pump and this would be hidden in a suitable place for protection or it would be put in the inside pocket of the coat. And boys would hold on to them for the night and guard them while they were dancing. There were some lads who never danced but stood there all night looking on. These lads would mind the pumps for the boys and girls while they were dancing and they'd often have five or six pumps in their possession.

Peaked caps were all the go that time and some lads never removed them when dancing. As the night wore on and the sets and barn dances were in full swing you'd see the boys turning back the caps and the peak of the cap would slope down their back. They'd then remove their jackets and roll up the sleeves of their shirts. This gave an indication of how heavy the going was, as did the sweat running down their faces. And I can tell you they'd be fair rubbing with the big white handkerchief for no visit to the dancehall was complete without displaying a big white handkerchief or a nice coloured one as the case might be and this was displayed on the top pocket of the jacket with a half yard of it hanging down. This showed great style and they'd go to all the rounds in the world to make sure that it was well folded and displayed. They'd have a big safety pin on the inside of the jacket stuck through the handkerchief to keep it in place. Some of the prime boys might give it a pull but faith! it would stay tight in the pocket. The girls would roll up the sleeves and remove their cardigans when the going was getting hot.

The boys would all cluster together at the back of the dancehall just inside the door and the girls would usually pack together around the cloakroom door like flies on a summer day. They'd move out when the music started and when finished they'd gently return back to the same position. This was the case at the beginning of the dance and all were very shy to start. But like horses when they'd get warmed up things would change. There was always a very slow start to see who'd take the floor first. So when the first pair would begin they'd all move out. As with cattle or sheep there was always one good leader and he'd get the rest of them going. As the night wore on the boys would move further into the dancehall and the girls would move to the seats by the wall on stools or long forms which were there for the comfort of the dancers when they wanted to rest. And usually when they'd get acquainted the boy would take the girl on his knee and oh! you'd never see such squeezing and hugging. The proprietor would move freely through the dancers keeping order, and he'd occasionally produce the big box of Lux flakes and sprinkle handfuls of them on the timber floor. This gave a good bite and slide for the dancers.

Waltzing and foxtrots were very orderly but when it

came to the set-dances you'd hear an occasional shout from the proprietor, 'No four-wheeling here!' as they'd usually create a bit of a rumpus. When two boys and two girls joined together there was a danger of a big spill. Some fellow might get a bit of a bump and he'd get his dander up; so order had to be restored fairly quickly. The boys would occasionally return to the cloakroom to have a look in the mirror and give the hair a bit of a comb – that's the ones who didn't wear the caps. No more than the hankies, the small pocket comb, better known as the rack, was also part of their toiletry and to accompany this they'd carry in their inside pockets a small bottle of hair oil known as Brilliantine which could be bought for twopence at the time. So a drop of this on the hand was rubbed into the hair, it was combed back and they were right again for the floor and another whirl. The jacket having been removed, the tie might now be taken off with the collar of the shirt. These would be folded nicely and put into the jacket pocket. Shirt sleeves freshly rolled up displayed their hairy hands and neck, giving a great display of strength.

The women would also be very active between dances in the cloakroom. Powdering and painting the rouge, as they called it, were very much the order of the night. Cosmetics were in short supply and a great man in those times was the red tea-bag. After the tea was emptied the red-coloured packet was kept by the servant girl and accompanied her to the dances. Indeed it was often passed around the other girls who might not have one. When the bag was damped and rubbed to the face it left part of its red colour on the cheekbones. A good daub of this on the dial would give them a grand blushing look like the sun going down and with a good dousing of powder they'd look like a mouse coming out of a flourbag. This made them very attractive to the boys. Eyebrows were also done in a most sophisticated way. A bit of a stick reddened in the fire and left cold was their ideal eyebrow pencil. This gave a great blackening to eyebrows, giving the appearance of a full moon. This piece of stick was always taken by the girls to the dances rolled up in a piece of paper, kept in an empty matchbox in case it would get damaged and placed in the compact bag with powder and lipstick. The same bag was not let out of the hand all night. A lot of this tiffin' up was done before they left the house. But since the girls had to cycle long distances in all kinds of weather some of this make-up would have vanished. When they'd arrive at the dancehall they'd have to replenish the dial again. After some lively dances, too, with perspiration running down their faces it would look like snow melting or a rainbow with the different colours mixing.

The boys in those times were like tick-tack men at races with one, two or three fingers up while dancing, booking future dances, and this confusion would go on all night. Indeed there were many high tempers when a girl didn't keep her promise. Many's the disappointed customer would approach the girl in question and say, 'You promised me this dance!' I can assure you there were a lot of fist fights but that was as far as they went. God love them, they'd square out to one another with the coats off and the cap pushed back. They were like young fighting cocks. The proprietor or floorman would rush in quickly to try and cool their tempers and then they'd say to each other, 'Come on outside!' which they did. A big crowd would follow and the two would beat the shit out of each other; and then it was all over and that was that. Of course there was many a black eye and bleeding nose. They'd return again to the dancehall but these lads were like prize bulls and they'd be watching each other all night. And maybe they'd have another go at each other outside on the road when the dance was over. There was always some interfering lad who'd urge them on. This was great fun and always a big audience gathered whether it was day or night.

While at these dances the servant boys usually kept with the servant girls. There would also be a good gathering of farmers' sons and daughters and a few workers from industries. They were there from all walks of life, though some of the farming people would not mix with the servants, which indeed was a great ridiculous class distinction. The majority of these working class were every bit as good as the ones that shunned them. As far as I and some of my pals were concerned we never turned our back on these poor people as they were the same in our eyes as any other boy or girl.

Indeed many a good farmer's son married a servant girl though it had to be a runaway marriage as they were blacklisted by the boy's family. When a thing like that happened it was a crime and they'd be whispering and talking about it for weeks. Some of these marriages turned out very well and lucky and they made great partners and great parents and did very well for themselves. They brought up great families who I have no doubt did very well for themselves and commanded very good positions. Marriages of that kind met all kinds of obstacles; the clergy were not in favour and it made things kind of hard for a boy and girl. The class distinction was stinking and the clergy were all for the big man though there might be the odd man of the robe who was fair and kind. But, thanks be to God, all that nonsense is done away with and gone we hope for ever.

Some of these halls were very primitive. I remember one which had neither a ladies' nor a gent's toilets. It was just a glorified barn with hanging lamps; so if you wanted to go to the toilet it was the case of going out around the corner and relieving yourself in the dark. With no light to direct him many's the man went out to relieve himself and was just about to do that when he'd hear a scream. A few women would be already there before him and on their haunches doing the same and already maybe after getting a fair sprinkling from some other lads. But all these things were taken in good spirits with no bad feelings. Such were the thrills of enjoyment in those days.

I remember one such dancehall out in the middle of nowhere. This contraption was owned by two brothers and it consisted of a good large shed with a partition off at one end for a gent's and ladies' cloakroom. The toilets were on the side of the hall, crude homemade yokes. Outside there was a running stream which never dried, summer or winter, and the toilets were built over this. There were four big poles stuck down on the ground for each toilet with an opening out from the dancehall. Around the poles were nailed a few sheets of galvanised iron to give a bit of privacy. Now in each toilet was a piece of wood about eighteen inches from the ground with a big round hole cut in it where the boy or girl could relieve themselves. The girls would naturally sit on these and there was a drop of about four feet between that and the running water. So it was ideal for the job, a natural flush.

Now from outside you could make your way into the dancehall through the toilet holes which many's the lad did as there was no fence or sheet iron on the bottom of the outside. A very large crowd from miles around would come to this dancehall whenever it was open. 'Twas a great attraction. Many prime boys used congregate outside in the summertime and they were up to all sorts of devilment. One evening some of these lads thought up a plan. One of them got a bunch of nettles and when the girl came to the toilet the buck was ready outside with a full view of what was happening. The minute she sat on the toilet up with the bunch of nettles and oh my God the screams! I can assure you it was a sore thing. The lads from inside used say it was a mighty howl to see the girl running into the dancehall with fright and her knickers around her ankles. The lads outside made their getaway as fast as they could. After those happenings the propriet- ors made sure they had the outside protected by boarding up the bottom of the toilets on the outside. A notice was placed on the ladies' toilet saying: 'All bottoms are not protected.'

11

CLASS DISTINCTION AND SUNDAY MASS

As I have mentioned in parts of this book class distinction was the greatest nonsense that ever existed. The farmer and his family always ate in the parlour, which was a distinguished room just down from the kitchen and usually kept in prime order for visitors; the boy and girl ate in the kitchen on an old rough table, or maybe in a back kitchen where pots and pans and buckets were kept. The family always entered the house by the front door whilst the servants had to use the back. Here in the rough-and-tumble back kitchen the unfortunate servants ate their meals and indeed the food was sometimes rough-and-tumble as well.

I was present at many a threshing of corn with the neighbouring farmers and witnessed the grip of class distinction when it came to mealtimes. The boss of the house would stand by the front door and the helping farmers and their sons would be directed into the parlour whilst the servant class would be directed to the back kitchen and no remarks passed. It was known that the food in the parlour was far better than in the back kitchen. Farmers usually had two or three days' threshing, especially in the big farms. Quite a lot of tillage was done and farmers within a few miles' radius helped each other. There'd be around thirty to forty men at each threshing. The farmers and servant boys worked hand-in-hand and were the best of friends but at dinnertime they were separated.

During the work in progress buckets of porter and jars would be taken around to the workers and mugs of porter handed out. Again the farmers and their sons were first on the list and poor servant boys left until last. I often felt like screaming when this would happen and there were other farmers' sons who felt likewise. Looking back I find it was a turning point in my outlook on life. Of course there were farmers and their sons who had this old daft notion of keeping up the practice and we used to feel so sorry for the poor servants; in the eyes of their employers they were nothing but slaves. In my eyes and those of my friends they were the salt of the earth and their bosses, the slave-drivers, were in our eyes just scum. Indeed it was very humiliating for the servants to be treated like cattle at a mart. Separating them at the kitchen door, sending the elite to the right and the rejects to the left – I sincerely hope that things are different in the next world.

Apart from being degraded at the parlour table they met the same fate while they were out socialising and even when going to Mass on a Sunday. They were all very good about the practice of their religion. In spite of all their hardship and suffering they went regularly to confession and communion. When attending the Sunday

Mass the parish priest or the curate would parade outside the church and of course he'd have a great nod or handshake for all the elite of the parish. Come the servant boy or girl they'd hardly be seen getting the occasional side-look. Of course, you'd be afraid of your life to say a word against them. We believed they could put a curse on you but that was the way we were brought up. What a change today, thanks be to God, although there still are a few old warriors around who feel the same as in the old days. In spite of all this the poor people went to Mass for God's sake and not for the priest's.

I remember down through the years when I got married, away back in the '40s. I got a job in County Waterford and met a very old priest whom I found to be very holy. We talked quite a lot. I told him about all this kind of treatment and how the servant class were treated and I distinctly remember his words to me were, 'May God forgive them; they were terribly wrong. I can tell you hell must be paved with the likes of those people who treated the poor like that.'

Usually on a Sunday morning in the spring and summer the servant boys would take the milk to the creamery. On weekdays the boss would go as there was other hard work for the boy to do on the farm. It was a very early start on Sunday mornings and they'd dress in their best to suit the purpose. Maybe a clean shirt and their best coat and their low shoes usually well polished. They'd usually wear just a mediocre trousers as the good one might get soiled whilst they were putting in the milk at the creamery. The good coat would be removed while this job was in progress and replaced again when the churns or creamery tanks were emptied. Then the horse or pony or the donkey was tied to a gate or a telegraph pole. The boy would then go to the early Mass which was at 8.00 am as he might not have the chance to go to the second Mass which was at 11.00 am. He had to wash churns when he got home as well as feed pigs and calves – his time was limited.

Since he was only half-dressed, as he would call it, with old and new clothes, he'd wait until all the rest were gone into the church. Then he and his pals, maybe thirty or forty of them, would enter the church and naturally they'd stay at the back with the rest of the ordinary people. I can tell you there were quite a lot of ordinary amongst the locals. They weren't all snobs or as we'd call them craw-thumpers that time. You'd never believe today the hat-lifting and cap-touching and bowing and bending to the local PP that there was in the country villages when he'd arrive on the scene. And of course many old PPs fattened on all this treatment, whilst at the back of the chapel the honest working men and women were deep in prayer, all with rosary beads.

There was one old priest who'd say first Mass every second Sunday and the curate who was a young man who would also say first Mass on a rotation system, so this gave the PP the chance of getting his turn at the watching game outside the front of the church. On Sundays whether he was saying first or second Mass he'd never give anyone a chance to stay in at the back of the church for this was the place where all the working lads stayed inside the door, especially the one who would be at the creamery.

There was always plenty of room up the front. As the well-to-do entered they always went up front, showing off their grandeur whilst the ordinary folk kept behind. They always hoped the priest wouldn't come down, for sometimes as soon as he had said the opening prayers he'd turn around and look down to the bottom of the church. Off with the spectacles and his vestments which he would lay on the altar. When the lads would see this it was like a stampede of cattle. All would start to move up front trying to squeeze into seats as near the back as possible but he'd keep pushing them like cattle being driven to a fair. It was embarrassing for the people but if there was a well-to-do person or a friend of his he'd turn a blind eye and let them stay there. He'd keep pushing and shoving and demanding in a good strong voice that they get up and keep moving. When this happened you'd always have the few who'd make their escape out the back door and run like March hares around the side of the church and say there until all was quiet. Then they'd come gently into the porch of the church and stay there. They daren't go home whether they be servant boy or small farmer.

The women were so devoted they'd be talking about getting the house consecrated if they thought they missed Mass on the stampede from the back of the church. There were two confessional boxes at the very back and these would be chock-full. I often saw people falling out of them and they hardly be able to close the door. His reverence would be wise to this and when he'd have the majority moved up he'd return to empty the boxes but the boys would be trying to hold the doors so as he couldn't open them. He'd keep at it and with shame they'd come out. Indeed it used to be a great laughing matter after.

I remember a small farmer coming into Mass in his old clothes after doing the creamery and whilst kneeling at the back he refused to move up for the priest so the priest said to him to get up or get out. So the man got up and walked out and from that day forward he never went to Mass again. Indeed every Sunday he'd drive the wife and family to Mass and wait outside for them until it was over. You might think that priest would ask him in or go and apologise but they never would bend to anybody.

When it came to receiving the sacraments the elite went up first and poor old Joe Soap had to await his turn at the end of the queue. The front seats were completely reserved for the very posh and in my time there were beautiful coloured kneeling cushions on the two front kneelers, supplied by the people who occupied them. There was many the good crack and laugh at some of the Masses. I remember at the beginning of the Second World War ordinary country people used to be afraid if a plane was heard overhead and there were many strayed over Ireland at that particular time. People used to be advised to run for shelter if the occasion ever arose and a few old women used to say that if they dropped a bomb on the chapel they'd all be killed – as if the plane pilot knew there would be a lot of people there. So on that note they were all advised to run for the sacristy at the back of the chapel. It was considered a safe sound building.

This old chat used to go on at night in the houses where the locals gathered. About this time there were new cottages built in our townland and a certain poor man, his wife and family got one and they were from an adjoining remote parish. So they were welcomed and visited by the local servant boys and girls as the old folks had sons and daughters also in service and of course this old chat went on about stray planes and what would happen. The old woman of the house took this very seriously. She didn't know much about our local Mass and the priest moving the boys up from the back of the chapel.

There was a local chap who was a bit wild and he had an old BSA motorbike and you'd hear it coming for miles away. This woman, being one of the grand old poor, used to wear a shawl going to Mass and she was settled down in one of the back seats, the shawl well wrapped around her head, the rosary beads out and praying hard with the eyes closed. The priest who looked down to the back of the church and saw the boys, turned around and stripped off the vestments as usual. She never noticed this and in the meantime the wild man on the motorbike came tearing into the village making a sound like a jet plane. He was always a bit late coming to Mass. The poor woman thought it was a plane and she said to the people beside her, 'God have mercy, we'll all be bombed', fearing the worst.

In the meantime the priest was on his way down from the altar to the rear of the church and at the same time all the lads went tearing up the aisle, some of them on their hunkers trying to hide their faces from the priest. When the old woman saw this she shot up like a hare and asked the first fellow she bumped into 'Is this a raid?' He thought she was referring to the priest and in a loud whisper he said, "Tis, Ma'am; and run for your life.' Off with the shawl, rolled it up in a ball and threw it on the seat and up the aisle on her hands and knees. When the priest was halfway down the church he turned back up to the altar as he knew the boys on the run would all come up the church. It was separated from the rest of the church by a nice railing with a little double gate. The priest had just gone in to the altar and closed the gate when the poor old woman came tearing up, opened the gate and right through the middle of the sanctuary into the sacristy and under the table.

Needless to say the priest was shocked and followed her in and of course she explained all to him and everything was ironed out and back to normal. Of course the boys at the back in their rush up the church saw all the carry-on and I can assure you there was giggling – specially from the ones in the confession boxes. But his reverence wasn't long straightening it out. He returned and put the run on the boys and there was some scattering. The antics of the woman had a good impression on a contrary priest and we all did believe it made a changed man of him. As he told some people after that, he felt very sorry for the humble old woman and from that day forward he very seldom bothered to come down from the altar to run the boys from the back of the church.

These were great moments of enjoyment and were talked about in many a house and at the crossroads for many a day after. These kind of capers were great fuel for the parish priest; he had no problem with sermons as when he got a hold of a few fellows in these circumstances he'd give it to them *gealtach* off the altar because when this man would get his tail up you could watch out for sparks. He would thunder that those pagans who had done the likes of this, especially abusing the confessional box, would never see the light of heaven. These were some of the ups and downs that the poor class had to put up with. Still they never turned away from their religion; as I said, they went for their faith and nothing else.

12

SPRING CALVING

Times on the farm got very busy and difficult in the spring as work piled up. It meant very early rising (around 5.00 am) for the boys and girls as cows were now starting to calf and these were times when the boy could be up all night keeping an eye on a sick cow, and there was no such thing as a rest next day. Instead when evening came he'd just make for the 'wad' [bed] immediately after the supper.

There was no such thing as calling the vet on those times as he'd waste money. And money to a farmer was his god and the nearest vet might be twenty miles away. Yes he'd be sent for in very urgent cases, if a quack failed to settle things. There were all sorts of quacks available in the old days. The most serious sickness at calving would be retaining the afterbirth. This was considered very serious by the farmer and if the cow retained this for a few days they would send for a vet if the quack failed. In olden times this was called the 'cleaning'. If you spoke of 'afterbirth' they'd be thinking you meant another calf. I've seen many a cure by quacks, some of them excellent, some weird, such as weights tied on to the afterbirth so that the cow would drop it. One of the best was the feeding of ivy leaves. These were collected off the bushes, trees and walls and fed in abundance, and they always had a good effect on the animal. The afterbirth was supposed to poison the animal if she retained it but the quack would declare that eating plenty of ivy would counteract the poisoning and indeed it did work.

There was a certain farmer whose cow held the cleaning so he decided to call in the vet who lived some twelve miles away and the way of contact was to send out a telegram. We'll call this man John Murphy. So John wrote the wording for the telegram on a piece of paper and sent the servant boy on his bike to the local post office. The farmer kept the wording as short as possible so it wouldn't cost much money. It read like this: 'Mr P. Cassidy, Vet. [not real name] Come quick, cow sick. John Murphy kept the cleaning.' Needless to say it was rightified by the post mistress. There were indeed many funny happenings around these times.

Red water was a very common disease and the great cure for this was Glauber Salts and porter, for usually after red water the beast got a form of constipation called murrain. The salt would be dissolved in warm water and mixed with a pint of porter or two, then this would be applied to the animal by bottling through the mouth. Some servant boys were excellent at this job as they had vast experience travelling each year from farm to farm and all would have been working from a youthful age with some very extensive farmers in different parts of the country. The stout or porter as they called it was bought by the gallon and at the price of a pint in those times it was far cheaper than to have to call in a vet. And the boy would always have a good swig for himself.

Porter was and is today a great beverage for any sick animal. I knew a boy was gifted at such cures and of course porter was his usual medicine. He was employed by a farmer who kept a few horses and he had one good one he used to run at the point-to-point races. As it happened this horse wasn't up to his form so the boy suggested plenty of porter. The boss agreed. It was a few weeks before the point-to-point and so the porter was applied in large quantities and on the day of the races the horse was in top form and won his race. Days after some other farmers were talking to the owner of the horse and of course they had known about the porter and one of them said to him, 'The porter is good.'

'Ah well,' he said, 'it must be excellent because Jack [that was the servant boy who was looking after the horse] ran the whole course with the horse.' So as the saying goes, he said, it's good for man or beast.

At the hiring fair in January some of the cute servant boys would ask the boss if he had good knowledge of cattle diseases and if the answer was yes they'd keep fishing around until they'd meet a client who would not be well up in that field. It was a great advantage to the boy to be well versed in all animal diseases for beside the extra drop of porter their services were eagerly required by other farmers. The word got around quickly that there was a good man in the locality and of course he'd earn an extra few shillings for rendering his services and he also commanded a good wage from his employer as a lot of responsibility would rest on him in connection with the health of the cattle. And I have seen some of these boys giving excellent service to adjoining farmers when there was a sick animal to be treated.

Often they'd be engaged in the evenings when their day's work was done in castrating bonhams, as all farmers kept quite a few breeding sows and this operation had to be carried out on little piglets from ages six to eight weeks old. This was a kind of professional job and they were well experienced at it. Likewise when the sow was giving birth to the bonhams they'd be there to nip off the teeth; piglets are fierce fighters and they'd cut each other when suckling and also cut the mother's teats and this would make her very irritable. Many farmers were not much good at these kind of skills but they made sure they learned many of their tricks from the servant boys. They were needed for sick pigs as they were a contrary lot to dose. They'd use a piece of a handle of a shovel or fork about three feet long with a rope looped through a hole in the end. This noose was put on the snout of the pig whilst the assistant would hold the ears. This loop would be given a few twists and the pig was now under complete control of the handler and the operator would apply the dose – not an easy task. But the boys were tops at this.

When castrating bonhams there were no proper utensils such as scalpels or lancing knives. The items used were just an old cast-off Mac's Smile razor blade dipped into a mug of disinfectant such as Jeyes Fluid or Lysol which were the in things at that time. The assistant would sit on a chair and hold the little pig between his knees whilst the operator did the necessary. When that was finished he'd put a pinch of salt on the wound. I can tell you they'd be some roaring but they never looked back and it always turned out to be an excellent job.

There was this small farmer who lived at the end of the locality where this servant boy was working and he heard about his great skills in helping sick cattle. So this evening he had a problem with a cow calving and he sent a messenger on a bike for this chap. The boy told the messenger that as soon as he had his work done he'd go on to see this cow. That servant boy used to tell this story many times. He said it was near dark when he arrived at this place after many enquiries since he had never met the man nor knew exactly where his house was. Anyway after travelling up an old boreen he arrived at an old farmhouse, went up to the door and knocked. A voice, that of an old woman, came from the corners of an old dark kitchen lit by a dim candle and asked 'Who is it?' And the boy said, 'I am the man come to see the sick cow.'

'Oh, God bless you! You're welcome. Go up the path there by the hedge; the young fellow is up there at the cowhouse with the cow.' So on he proceeded up to the cowhouse, hoping the young fellow was there. Again an old dim light and when the servant boy got near his heart filled with fright when from the back of the cowhouse a voice said, 'Did you meet my mother?' Lo and behold in the dim light he saw an old man who appeared to be very feeble and looked as if he hadn't cleaned himself for years. This was the young fellow that the old woman was referring to! Of course the old people always referred to their sons and dependants as the young ones, especially any of those who remained with their parents on the farm and I expect that this poor unfortunate remained to look after the mother. This practice prevented a lot of country people from getting married in those days.

Nighttime in the spring was as busy as daytime, for the servant boys could be seen at any hour moving around the farmyard with his storm lantern. When the cow started to calf they'd give her time and if it happened to be a big calf which could cause a bit of trouble – they knew by the size of the front legs and a little handling to feel the head – they always had a handy pair of short ropes available with loops on the ends steeped in a bucket of disinfectant. They'd slip them on the legs when they'd appear and give a little help. Sometimes this didn't work and then they might have to get extra help from a neighbouring farmer if it was a tough birth, especially with a heifer in her first calf. I was present at many of these calvings. One man would be in command and it was like a tug-of-war. He'd be watching the cow for movements of pain and forcing and when he'd see this he'd shout to the man on the ropes, 'Heave to; pull, ye devils, pull!' – and it worked. Sometimes there would be a problem with a big bull calf when the hips got stuck. I knew an experienced servant boy who had an excellent trick for this: he'd get all the men pulling to turn the animal over from one side to the other and the calf came out without any trouble. I have never seen this to fail. And down through the years I have shown this to many's the farmer and no one I met had ever heard of this trick. It goes to prove that good servant boys left their skills throughout the country farms.

When the calf was born the cow would lick it till it was

dry and the boy would also give a little help by brushing the calf with handfuls of hay. The calf would then be removed to another house and not left to suckle the mother. The farmers in those times thought it best to remove the calf because if it were left too long with the mother she'd get too fond of it and wouldn't let down her milk for a few days. So a few hours after calving, the milk was taken from the mother. This first milking was called beastings and was fed in turn to the newborn calf.

This feeding was important and a big job which required expertise as the newborn calf is very unsteady on its feet. You held the bucket in one hand, had hold of the calf by the head with the other and tried to get a finger into its mouth to make it take the milk. Sometimes the boy would hold the calf between his legs. This operation could take twenty minutes to a half-hour for the first feed. It was important to get two to three pints of beastings into the newborn as soon as possible as it prevented infection and scouring. There would be the same carry-on for two days or so, until the calf would eventually take the milk by himself.

I often heard the lads saying, 'Put plenty of milk in the bucket!' for by the time the calf had its share taken there'd be half of it spilled from puking; there'd be as much milk on the feeder's trousers as in the calf's belly and this used to give rise to the stench you'd get from the overalls they'd wear for protection. If they had a chance when finished their day's work they'd give the overalls a good washing and hang them out to dry in the hayshed. If the weather was kind to them they would hang them out on a bush or hedge. If they were lucky enough

to have a spare pair of overalls they'd change into them.
Few of them were in that position and indeed their
sleeping quarters often had a very strong aroma from
leaving these clothes around the room for a few days until
they'd get the chance to wash. Especially in the warm
weather you'd get a quare smell.

Milking cows was now in full swing and it meant an
early start to get the milk off to the creamery. Milk was
important; this was the product or say the raw material
that the farmer mostly depended on.

At the milking the boy went through the same messing
as he did when feeding calves. With some cross cows,
especially heifers, milking for the first time was difficult.
They were contrary and fierce kickers, and the boy was
bound to get some milk on his clothes. For his protection
he wore a bag apron. This was made out of twenty-stone
meal bags which were plentiful at the time and they were
fairly long and big. A hole was cut on the bottom and on
the sides also, the bottom hole for the head, and the
hands out through the sides. A string of bag twine was
tied around the waist so that the boy was now fully
protected from spattering milk. The apron was also a
protection from cow manure, of which there was never
any shortage. With the tail flying every way like a blade
of a helicopter you'd little chance of escaping a good
spraying of cow dung. Sitting on a three-legged stool with
the bucket between his legs and a cap turned back, the
boy was fully ready for any assault or rough treatment
and indeed he got a lot of it.

I was often present during these milkings and you'd
hear the boys like the lark in the clear morning air in full

song, for some of the lads were a dab hand at singing and they used to say this was a great way to soothe the animal and help her to let down a good supply of milk and quickly at that. Of course as the spring progressed and the cows and heifers were milked morning and evening, the cross ones would be settling down and getting more timid. You'd still get the odd nervous one who'd give you the leg unexpectedly, and not alone would you get a kick but they'd lift the leg as quick as a flash and land it right into the bucket of milk and spill the lot of it. The boys were canny lads and with a cross cow they'd put a spare bucket out on the passageway and every now and again they'd empty their milking bucket into this as soon as they'd have a pint or two. If then the leg landed in the bucket there wouldn't be much to spill.

I encountered some bad kicking cows in my time and often you'd be driven out into the passageway. The boys had their own way of explaining about cross heifers. They used say the wildest of boys makes the best of old men and the crossest of heifers would make the best of old cows. Another trick to control kickers was with a spancel. This was done by tying a piece of rope around the cow's legs just below the hocks so when she'd go to lift the leg she hadn't full control of it while it was tied to the other one. But the cows did not take kindly to this. This tail also had to be tied to one of her legs with a bit of twine for where you had kickers or cross cows they would fire loose manure with temper and if the tail was loose your face and clothes would be like a slurry pit covered all over with, as the boys used say, sweet violets. The perfume of this in warm weather was unbearable.

I have often seen bad-tempered cows or heifers break loose from their tying when they were spancelled and going daft, out of the cowhouse into the field with the rope well tied around their back legs. I can tell you that it took some running to get them back in and remove the rope and try to finish milking them. It was very bad to leave milk to a cow or heifer especially after calving, as they could develop milk fever. This was very prevalent in those times of hard milking especially with heavy milking cows, and this took some curing with old quack cures. Again the vet was the last resort and the handy servant boy with the good cures was always on call.

There was one such farmer who had a very sick cow so he sent for this servant boy who came immediately, around dinnertime. He gave her the treatment and warned the farmer to make sure that the cow got up from lying down for if she stayed down too long she'd not improve. Time dragged on and the cow wouldn't rise so the farmer sent for the boy again in the evening. When he arrived the cow which was in a house by herself, looked well but wouldn't rise. The farmer and the wife were at the door looking in and the old woman was *casaoideach* [complaining] about the poor cow. She had with her an old sheepdog who was now retired and he'd always be around the kitchen and hardly able to walk but he'd follow the old woman everywhere. So he was also at the door beside the old woman where the cow was. The boy just stood at the door and the farmer said, 'What do you think we'll do to get her up?' The boy never said a word only turned around fast, caught the old dog by the back of the head and rump and threw him like a shot at the cow's head and she got up like a flash of lightning. The old dog came out of the house and the roar of speed of him was like a shot out of a gun and never in his life had he run so fast. The poor old woman nearly died but the boss roared out laughing. The cow got better. The boys always had their tricks and they worked.

After the milking came the job of taking the milk to the creamery. As they used say this was a very cushy job and it was usually the boss who would do this. While times were busy on the farm the boy remained behind, did the feeding of the animals and then to the fields when he was finished, preparing for sowing the crops. Of course if it was a wet morning the boy was sent to the creamery so there was no danger that the governor would get himself wet. The boy would enjoy this in spite of getting wet as he'd have a great chance to meet up with his friends, especially the lassies, as quite a lot of servant girls went to the creamery. Brilliant they were at the job, fully capable of handling horse, pony or jennet as the case maybe. Dressed in rough clothes and strong hobnail boots and black ribbed stockings, they were well able to handle the twenty-gallon tank when it arrived at the stand where the milk was taken in. And of course the boy would be jumping to help them, especially if there was a good-looking girl in question. There he'd be, throwing off the coat, rolling up the sleeves and helping the girl's every need, showing himself off as a future partner – and it worked sometimes.

Some of these girls were very witty and great sport. In those times an inspector would arrive at the creamery to inspect the milk and churns for hygiene, although God knows there was very little of it at the time. Anyway the inspector was on the milk stand fully graced in a snow-white coat and very precise, no chat. This lady took off the covers and he tested the milk that was OK. 'Now,' he said, 'please turn up the churns till I inspect the bottom.' Quickly and abruptly he said to her, 'Your bottoms are very dirty.'

'Well, sir,' she said, 'if all our bottoms were turned up there'd be very few clean ones.' He just turned and smiled. There were many good cracks like that.

13

SPRING SOWING

Back on the farm, preparation was in full swing for tillage crops. The drill would be made and opened for sowing potatoes and root crops and it was a pleasure to see the skills of some of these lads who were not overfed, badly clothed and wearing maybe bad old boots. The heaps of manure that were in the farmyard had to be drawn out to the field and spread on the drills for planting the crops. Usually adjoining farmers would share their servant boys during the busy season. There would be some hectic action. Three or four horse-and-carts would draw out the farmyard manure, which had to be hand-forked with the four-pronged pike. All worked hard and long hours and moved quickly. I can tell you it didn't take them long to remove that farm dung.

When the manure was taken out to where the tillage crops had been sown, it had to be spread nice and evenly on the drills, which was a technique in itself. To add hardship to it the boys had to walk on the dung between the drills so as to make it nice and flat for closing. There was very little fertiliser used in those days; it was mostly organic crops. It's no wonder there was so little disease or running to doctors.

The root crops and potatoes would get a little dressing of fertiliser. I remember myself mixing these as if it were yesterday. You'd mix three bags of phosphate and one of potash with a half-bag of sulphate of ammonia. All bags then were two hundredweight [100kg] heavy; yet the strong lads of the time had no hesitation in swinging them up on their backs. These were spilled out on a concrete floor or if the weather was dry they were mixed out on the farmyard. The mixture had to be put out immediately on the crop ground; left lying in the bags it would get like concrete. This was applied by hand from a bucket. Hail, rain or snow, this had to be used immediately after mixing, and if there were any small boys like myself around it would be our job to keep the spreaders supplied. We'd be running with small buckets to them like the hares and of course there was a reward for us at the end of the day. A few pence from the boss was a godsend in those bad times.

I remember helping a local farmer with the crops one season and at the end of it all he followed me out after giving me the tea and in the quiet when nobody could see him he handed me this parcel. There was as much paper and twine around it you'd think it was being posted to America. He thanked me for being such a good boy and a great help to him and his boys and said he'd bought this present for me. I took it and thanked him and went on my way home. But as soon as I got out of sight I sat down by a fence and opened the parcel and lo and behold! when all was removed there to my surprise was a span-new hurley stick. You'd swear I had won the Sweep. I was so overjoyed with this that I didn't want to dirty it hurling. The cost was about one shilling and sixpence but to me it was something special as we could never afford to buy a hurley. Our method of getting one was to go out and cut a lump of ash tree and we'd give up nights and days of dressing this with probably a bad old axe. The final process was planing it down with pieces of broken bottles, which was a special trade in itself. There were no planes or sandpaper available as all these things cost money. Still we were happy and content with our lot as we didn't know any better.

There was no fertiliser used for corn, only the dung that was put out in the spring on the unploughed land. This dung would usually be a few years old and well rotted so it would plough well into the soil. Barley and oats could be sown without dung but wheat required more nourishment as it was a cash crop and part of the farmer's income. Like the fertiliser the corn was sown by hand. The sower had a bag tied around the waist which held about a stone of corn. This had to be spread evenly and a good man could sow three or four acres a day. These in turn were covered over by horses and harrow. The potatoes were also sown by hand. There could be ten people sowing, including men and women who were hired in for a few days. This indeed was a back-breaking job. The boss did no planting but kept an eye on the workers and kept up the crazy old call: 'Keep the eyes up!' There was then the belief that if the eyes of the potatoes were not turned up they wouldn't grow well.

Before the planting of potatoes there was the task of

getting the seed ready. This entailed the cutting of the *sceallán*. The small seed potatoes were passed on as suitable for planting but the big ones were split into two or three parts according to size. This work was usually done by women, mainly those poor people living in the adjacent villages. They'd arrive well wrapped up prepared for the cold, wearing a good plaid shawl.

The cutting would be done in a big open shed or maybe the haybarn. The potatoes would be brought in bags and dumped out on the floor. The women would half-fill a bag of hay and use this to kneel on, and well equipped with good sharp knives proceed to cut the *sceallán*. This could take a week or more according to the amount required for sowing.

The woman would be paid by the bag or heap of potatoes. Twenty or thirty bags were dumped for cutting and as she cut they were pitched back separated. They weren't bagged until the boss had checked them for size. A good worker could earn up to thirty shillings per week at this sort of work and that was considered excellent pay in those times. It was extra money for the housewife while the husband would be employed by some other farmer. Cutting *sceallán* was a severe yoke on the hands. The woman would usually wear a leather band around the palm of the hand to prevent it from getting sore. This leather band would be a piece of an old boot, from the upper or maybe the tongue if it was wide enough. Otherwise she used a piece of an old rubber tube which could be got from a garage.

If the weather was fine the cutting would be done at the face of the pit where the praties were stored out in the haggard (a little field beside the farmyard). This would spare a lot of labour since it did away with drawing to the shed and bagging. If the farmer or his wife had a kind heart they give the woman her dinner and tea with the rest of the servants. Otherwise she'd have to bring her own grub with her, a pint bottle or two of tea and a few cuts of bread. The bottles would be put into a few old discarded socks belonging to the man and this would help to keep them warm. The women would tell you to cut with a full belly. I knew some women who'd bring their children with them to help and again they'd tell you it was to get a decent bit to eat for the children. God knows it's no wonder that their offspring emigrated to do better for themselves (which they did) when they saw what their parents suffered to try and survive and make a bit of a living.

I remember one old woman who was a *sceallán*-cutter all her life and she used to smoke the clay pipe. She'd have a mixture of tobacco, tea and old butts of cigarettes. Tea was a great go in those times as it was cheaper than tobacco. And, as I have said, sometimes beet pulp was used in the mixture. I often thought we'd smother when she lit up this concoction; the stench of it was terrible. God love her she'd be in the stitches laughing at us and she lived to a ripe old age. We'd all help to try and get bits of tobacco for her. She used to tell us how she got into smoking. She was the youngest of a family of fifteen and as a girl growing up she used to help to fill the pipe for her father who was a cripple with pains. That's how she got hooked on smoking. (In those times there was nothing for pains especially for poor people only old quacks, using all sorts of old rubs. Today we'd call it arthritis.) These *sceallán*-cutters would also help at the sowing of the potato crop for there was one thing sure: they were certain of a good dinner at the farmer's table. Again we came up against the age-old story of class distinction when it came to going in for the dinner: poor to the left and gentry to the right.

It must be said that there were the odd few farmers who had the boys and girls at their own family tables. These were just medium-sized farmers who possibly had young boys or elderly men or else girls as servants. These got good treatment, were well fed and bedded, many in a settle bed in the kitchen or in one of the back rooms. But the wages these farmers could afford to pay were small. So it was that the good strong hard-working boy or girl went for the big farmer and the big wages although the treatment might not be so good. It was the money that counted.

14

THE SUMMER SEASON ON THE FARM

The summer day's pattern was: up early, have a quick bite and proceed to collect the cows who would be now out at grass. The boy would tackle up the pony or horse to the cart, put on the milk tanks, four or five of them, each holding twenty gallons, the milking buckets and a nice piece of muslin for straining the milk, which would be rolled up in a piece of paper to keep it clean.

Accompanied by the dog or dogs he'd go to the field where the cows were. This could be a long ways from the farmyard. He'd call the cows, who would already be rounded-up into a corner of the field as they were well used to this when they were out for day and night grazing. It was interesting to see this kind of training, for when the cows saw the horse and cart and churns coming they'd all gather into a corner and stand there like statues waiting to be milked. Maybe five or six milkers, both boys and girls, would be engaged in the job, possibly having to milk up to eighty cows between them. They'd don their bag aprons, equipped with a three-legged stool and a piece of rope in case they had a kicker – of which there were many – and also a piece of twine to tie the tail. In summer weather with plenty of grass the cows would be fairly loose in their manure and with flies annoying them they'd be swishing their tails. I can assure you you'd have a dirty face. The tail would be tied to the cow's leg and this kept things under control.

During the milking out season there were many wet mornings and evenings but wet or no wet the cows had to be milked. Once milking out in the fields started, the cows would not be brought into the house in the farmyard until the beginning of winter. The idea of milking out was to save labour and keep the farmhouses and yard tidy.

For protection against the bad weather the milkers wore the bag apron and also contrived a bag for the head. This was done by doubling in the corners of the mealbag and placing it on the head. But no matter how much protection you had you were bound to get wet on the sleeves of the coat for you could be sitting for over an hour in heavy rain. Still the milkers survived although they may have stayed all day in these damp clothes until they'd change in the evening.

Now that the cows were out there'd be plenty of time for tidying up around the farmyard. Houses would be cleaned out as they were fairly dirty after the long winter. Inside would be whitewashed with maybe a bit of painting done to the timber-work. Weeds around the farmyard would be cut and burned. And then there was that very popular job, picking stones off the fields, especially meadows.

Plenty of dung from the yard would have been spread on these meadows and plenty of stones would appear. You'd often wonder from year to year where all the stones would come from. These would be picked by hand into a bucket and placed in little heaps on the field. It was a laborious back-breaking job and it's no wonder that in later years so many of these unfortunate men suffered from pains of all sorts from hardship and wettings.

There would also be plenty of fences to be repaired while thorn hedges would be neatly cut and laid along the top of the fence to control the cattle. Very little barbed wire was used as this was considered a great danger to stock, to milking cows especially.

The root crops that were sown in the spring would now be coming in for some care. It took miles of walking after the horse to scuffle between the drills with an implement called a scuffler. The root crops and potatoes would get a good doing with this to check the weeds that grew between the drills. Then there was the hand-weeding and thinning of turnips, mangolds and maybe sugar beet which was a great cash crop for most farmers. This thinning was a severe, tedious job especially in warm weather at the end of May and during June and July. Like tending the cows it had to be done wet or fine with pieces of bags tied around your knees. You'd do some praying for a few weeks! I can assure you you'd be fairly sore and stiff in the legs and hands, and in wet weather there'd be lumps of clay hanging on to your clothes.

When you'd reach the end of the drill you'd take a break for a few minutes as some of these drills were up to 600 yards long. You'd stop for a smoke as usually all boys loved their old fag. This was a verbal agreement with the boss that you rested for a few minutes at the end of each drill. Although he might not be there in the field watching you, he wouldn't be far away. The boys always felt uneasy if they stopped before they reached the end. The boss might well be in the next field peeping through the bushes and if he noticed a slacking in the work he'd let the boys know fairly quickly with a loud roar. You may be sure this was obeyed. While the boys were all wearing bags as protection on wet days the boss hovered at the end of the field in the shelter. He might have a big umbrella for protection, and he'd occasionally move down through the drills and point out any spots that were not properly done.

Stopping for a smoke was a bit of a luxury, the fags lit, as I have said, from a sod of turf smouldering in an old tin or bucket turned sideways to keep it dry. Matches were used as little as possible in the field. They were kept for the evening when the boys went for a stroll. Again they might not have the price of the box of matches and they used say that the fags lit from the sod of turf made a lot sweeter smoke and, besides, that sod of smouldering turf would last all day. They'd just pick up the turf from the container, give it a few puffs with their mouth and they were in business with a perfect cigarette lighter.

Women and children from the poor families were employed at the thinning too and were capable of earning a few handy shillings. They were paid by the drill, hard-earned money, God help us.

After a rough old day weeding and thinning you'd still have to face the milking and feeding of the yarded stock. But after all this hardship when the supper was over the boys and girls were up and gallant and ready to move out for the evening stroll.

15

Hurling Matches and Sunday Sports

Moving out for their evening's entertainment in the summertime the boys and girls would probably go to the old country hurling fields which were plentiful in those times. There could be fifty or sixty lads there, from farmers' sons to creamery workers, lads from the village and servant boys and a good audience of onlookers of both sexes.

The field was usually on the side of the road where they all congregated and indeed that was the place where, thank God, there was no class distinction. All would line out in a great friendly manner and usually a match would be played, a good game of hurling with fifteen a side. A reasonable good man or two was selected to pick the teams and they usually mixed them up very well. Both farmers' sons and servant boys were on the same side. This was done for the spotting of good players and indeed many's the good servant boy turned out to be an excellent hurler or footballer.

The playing pitch was sometimes a crude field maybe grazed by cattle. It was the generosity of some kind-hearted farmer that let us have a field and occasionally at the height of the hurling season we might be shifted to another field as the one we were playing on was required for meadow. The boys would be busy at times, shifting goal posts and digging holes and putting bits of sticks for markers. The lime brush and bucket were in full use marking squares around the goals and the centre-field and sides. This would be a rushed job but considering there'd be twenty or thirty lads at it, it didn't take long.

Markings created great excitement as there were regular disputes about what was right. Some supposed expert would be called on to measure and re-measure, and since no tape was available the bounds had to be walked yard by yard. It often happened that a second and third pacer was called in. This was usually done by the older men and indeed some of them were very contrary; you'd swear it was playing for an All-Ireland final we were with the goings-on of them. Then a length of rope would be produced to measure the goal posts. It was a howl at times: 'Shift that one in a few inches or out a few inches . . . ' and then you had the genius standing at one of the posts with one eye shut and he taking stock to tell if they were on line. Then you'd have some prime boy who'd give one of the poles a shift and you were back to square one. You might have a congregation assembling and stating they were crooked to rise the old men, and indeed sometimes they got very vexed. But, as the old saying used go, after long and painful sitting everything was in order. There was a crossbar made of a crude kind of a long pole or maybe two tied together. These would be supported on six-inch nails hammered into the upright and tied with a piece of twine to keep them in place.

Now the lads would be assembled in the centre of the field to prepare for the start and the call would go out for handkerchiefs and a man to umpire on each side of the goalposts. A coloured handkerchief was used to signal a goal and a white one for a point. There were also men on the sides with white handkerchiefs to signal sideline balls. There was often a scarcity of handkerchiefs and there might be the occasional shirt used for a signal. It was any port in a storm. Sometimes there might be a big strong man in the goals and with an overhead ball coming in he'd jump up and catch the crossbar and pull it down crashing. And then there would be some disputing whether to declare a goal or a point. Some senior citizens got very serious about this affair and it would be talked about for a few days after at the creamery and the crossroads.

And then there were the *sliotair* which were the balls used for hurley and a collection of a few pence from each individual would be secured for the purchase of these. It was always good to have a replacement in case one or two got lost. There were always big whitethorn ditches in these fields and with big rough lads playing they were capable of hitting the ball anywhere and as they'd say themselves: 'When I'll hit the ball I'll give it all my power!' – and they had some power.

The *sliotar* was made of leather and if you happened to get a shot of this in the face or any other part of your body you wouldn't forget it. When these matches would drag on until dark they often ran out of *sliotair* and wouldn't have time to look for them until the following evening. So you'd never seen such commotion making a ball of rags and bags and winding twine around it. Sometimes they'd take the laces of some poor unfortunate man's boot to try and finish this match. Since some of the lads were fairly rough you'd sometimes see more sods than balls flying, especially in the kind of fields they'd be playing on with their tufts of grass and rushes.

Come Sunday, it was a very special day, as championship matches and challenge games were widely played. The match might be held in our local hurling field or in some other parish but it was always exciting looking beforehand for a field suitable for the Sunday game and convenient to the village if possible. The search often went on late into Saturday night before a suitable pitch was secured from some decent farmer. Money was out of the question at that time although some country clubs had their own pitches rented at a small fee from some generous landowner. There'd be some running then on late Saturday night or early Sunday morning getting goalposts and marking out the pitch with fresh lime. Then there might be a chance of getting some kind gentleman to lend us a pair of horses and mowing machine to trim the pitch, as in the summer time all pastures were overgrown. This would have to be cut and gathered and bundled up on the sideline, where afterwards it made a grand soft seat for some of the spectators. God help any one who mistakenly sat down on the lines of fresh lime especially on a warm Sunday. I can assure you when they got on their feet they had the map of Ireland painted across their arse.

They came from miles around on bicycle and foot to these hurling matches. The visiting teams would arrive in lorries with creels on the side protecting them from falling out. These old lorries would accommodate fifty or sixty people standing and packed like sardines, and the driver might have seven or eight young fellows with him in the cab. Many's the time I travelled in these old lorries; the going was all right but the coming home . . . especially for the winning team, as after the match they retired to the public houses and didn't leave until all hours of night and you'd hear the *calabairt* for miles. They'd all be in full song murdering 'The Rose of Tralee'. I often thought after it was the only song they knew at the time and it would be like a bird show with every man trying to break into his own song.

At the matches all types of hawkers would be there, selling all types of comestibles: ice cream, apples, oranges and the famous Peggy's Leg which was a kind of a long thick brown sweet. They all had their own kind of a tent to protect them from rain or sunshine. The women paraded the ground, well equipped with plaid shawls and holding their wares in wicker baskets. You'd hear their loud calling distinctly, 'Apples, oranges, bananas, choco-late . . . ' You'd get a handful of nice rosy apples for a penny and the same for Peggy's Leg.

There'd be some stuff sold at these matches. The hawkers usually travelled by pony and sidecar though the poorer ones would have a good big Spanish ass to haul their belongings. Admission to these matches was about sixpence, a hard amount to get at the time. Knowing the country lads I am sure that the majority of them came in over the fences. It was hard to control them and try and direct them to the entrance gate where the money was collected. Though there would be a good few stewards keeping control at the fences, occasionally they'd turn a blind eye if some friend they knew was coming in over the fence.

The teams usually togged out quite respectably for these matches, with team jerseys and togs which were specially washed for the occasion. None of these togs would have been bought in a shop. They were homemade of calico or the good old flourbag. The bags would be washed and rewashed to get them in spick order for making the togs, and when they *were* made the majority of them still carried their brand on the back, such as Sunrise Flour, and always across the arse was the weight, 140 lbs, which some of the players were recognised by. These matches often turned into terrible brawls which sometimes ended up in the local pub or dancehall and just like a war they often went completely out of control. The players would line up in the middle of the field with hurleys raised ready for a major onslaught, but with the help of stewards and onlookers they'd be partly controlled and separated until tempers cooled and the match would be started again.

At half-time there was a break for approximately ten minutes and oranges then were the order of the day. The old hawker woman would hand over the basket at a price to the captain of the team or preferably to somebody not playing but in charge of the teams. Each member of the team got a few to quench the thirst and you'd have the few young boys congregated around the players in the middle of the field watching for the occasional orange which might be passed around.

There were no changing-rooms in those times; the players stripped off in the corners of the field, one team to the left, the other to the right. You rolled your clothes and shoes up in a lump and handed them to the men who were appointed to keep an eye on them. You just had to hope that every man would get his own when the match was over. Of course, when the match would get lively and exciting the men in charge would completely forget about the boys' clothes. If you had money and fags you'd have to give them to a friend to look after them; otherwise you could be fairly short at the end of the day.

The Sunday sports always turned out to be a day of great enjoyment. These were held all over the country. Every town and village had its own entertainment, with every kind of trickster attending these venues. You had the Three-Card-Trick man, who'd command a great audience, the throwing of the rings, the diamond board which was on the ground with the hawker's loud shriek of, 'Two on black, three on white and five on the crown', and then there was Rickety Kate which was an upright circular wheel with numbers marked on the rim and separated by nails. This was spun around and a light wire handle with springs on it would stop at a number held by the nails. On a table beside the wheel there was a big cloth with numbers corresponding to those on the wheel. You might win a few pence on this and more than often you lost what you had. We always got broke at this and indeed it wasn't hard at that time to get broke as our finances were very small but we had a great old love for this kind of game. The spinner always came out the winner.

But of all the sideshows the one which gave the most

enjoyment and attracted the biggest crowd was the Man in the Barrel. It consisted of an ordinary forty-gallon timber barrel and the guy would stand inside it. About eight inches from the top was a hole cut the size of an old penny. Now you got five balls for a penny and these, about the size of a hurling ball, were made of solid timber. The trick was to hit the man in the barrel on the head, standing at a distance of twenty feet away, and you got five free balls if you did this. You usually held the spare balls in your left hand and threw with the right. But of course no one was able to hit this man for as fast as you would throw the ball he would duck down and peep through the hole in the barrel in case you were coming quickly with the next ball. When he'd see everything was clear he'd come up fast again.

But there was a certain chap who was a terrific shot with his left hand (a left-handed person was known as a *ciotóg*). He got the five balls and put four of them in the left hand and started to throw with the right, not giving away his secret. The man in the barrel didn't know he was a *ciotóg*. He threw the first one with his right hand and, of course, he missed his target. The same with the second, the third and fourth ball. The fifth was still in the left hand and the man in the barrel came up quickly, thinking he was transferring it to the right hand. Instead as soon as the thrower saw his eye move from the peephole and the hair of the head begin to appear over the top of the barrel, he let fly and struck him right on the forehead. The onlookers went wild with laughter and I can assure you the man throwing the balls didn't ask for five free ones. He made a hasty escape or there would have been blue murder.

There were many such good cracks. There was the one known as the fat lady, called one of the seven wonders. There was great excitement to see this marvel, which was housed in a good-sized tent with admission twopence. There was a queue to get in, and poles and a rope a few feet out from the tent were used to keep back the crowd. Seven people were admitted at one go. Inside there was a dull kind of a light and a chap sitting in the corner playing a banjo. Each person had his own kind of a cubicle and you put your arms on a kind of a counter and a long board was lowered down behind your back and shoulders so you couldn't move, though you could plainly see the other people who were in the tent with you. Inside this counter the floor was raised a few feet and the man playing the banjo would walk around the inside raised floor. Although you'd be kind of locked up in your little holder you'd be looking at him and them he'd retreat to the end of the tent and announce, 'One of the seven wonders!' The light would get brighter and he'd play the banjo louder and from behind a curtain emerged a huge fat woman dressed in scanty clothes.

She walked around the raised floor and gently moved in towards the onlookers, who couldn't move back or sideways, and she'd pull her knickers down and rub the two cheeks of her arse across your mouth. She'd do that a few times and, needless to say, they'd be roars and cursing and spitting and some fellows trying to bite her. But after a few minutes she disappeared back behind the curtains and an attendant came out to relieve the onlookers, asked them how they enjoyed it. They were asked not to tell the others outside but to let them be caught the same as they were, and all would agree. When they came out they'd be wild enquiring to know what it was like and of course they were assured it was wonderful. So in went more and more people without any of those waiting to come in being any the wiser.

Such was the excitement and entertainment in those times long ago. People's entertainment was limited, unlike the present times. These occasions were a complete treat and joy to everybody, especially the working class who had to make their own enjoyment. And no matter what that enjoyment was, they always had to return in the evening to the milking of the cows, which would be held over until later than usual to accommodate the servant boys and girls seeing it was a special occasion.

When they arrived at their destination they'd get a quick cup of tea, put on the old working clothes and it was back to business as usual. The old cup of tea was a welcome guest in these times as there was no money for refreshment with the exception of the bottle of lemonade and a bun. If it happened to be an outdoor event conveni- ent to the village they might have a bottle of Guinness or two. Many's the good servant man returned late in the evening and had to face into milking straight away without any bit to eat until the evening's work was done. They were well used to this long fasting, having been brought up in very poor conditions and coming from big families. As many of the lads would tell you, in their youthful days they saw more dinnertimes than dinners. So the job was number one priority and had to be pro- tected, and as the poor were plentiful and so were servant boys and girls, a foot could not be put wrong and the farmers knew this and played on it.

In spite of all this, when milking and all the necessary chores were done, the boy would eat a good supper and then he was ready up and off, cleaned like a new pin with his best Sunday wear and out for the night. Come to think of it, these lads and lassies had hearts like saints.

16

THE TRIP TO FOYNES

On one occasion I was involved with a servant boy who lost his job for not returning to his work on a Sunday evening and, God help them, there was no union or farmworkers' body to protect them in those days. It happened as a result of an outing to Foynes in County Limerick where the seaplane, the Yankee Clipper, was to land. At the time this was all the local news and strange to us. People from all around the district were thrilled with excitement to hear of this great wonder when word got around that the Yankee Clipper would be at Foynes on the Sunday afternoon. So a few of us decided to go and see it. It was the month of July in the late '30s, a busy time of the year for farmers. We had in our company a few servant boys who were game for anything. It was a long journey, about thirty-two miles, so with our jobs done and the milk delivered to the creamery we got early Mass, had a quick breakfast and mounted our bicycles.

We set off on our journey and in our own right we were lords of the road, happy as Larry, with a few extra bob in our pockets. We were like the mountain lark, free as the air, as if we owned the whole world. It was nonstop until we got to Foynes, where there was quite a big crowd of people there who had travelled long and short journeys. They had come cycling, walking, travelling by ass-cart, horse-trap and quite a few sidecars which were very popular for transport among the well-to-do who could afford them.

When we arrived we heard to our disappointment that the Clipper would not be arriving until Monday. We took it in our stride and accepted the news in good faith; of course we had no other choice. A few of us who could afford it decided to stay on for the day and make the best of a bad lot. The servant boys who had to return for the evening's milking couldn't wait but one wild lad decided he'd chance his arm and wait on for the evening. He said he'd come up with some good excuse.

We fooled around for the day. There were plenty of amusements although we had little money. We did, however, have something to eat as there were plenty of eating-houses as we called them. Restaurants were not heard of in those times. You'd get plenty of tea, bread and butter and maybe a bun for a shilling and sixpence. That kept you happy for the day with maybe the odd bottle of lemonade. On windows of eating-houses there were notices written with white paint: tea and ham 2/6 – out of our reach so we were thankful for small mercies. For us it was a great day's enjoyment and we decided to stay on for a few hours in the evening as the day was beautiful with a good long bright evening. Later we heard that there was a carnival in Adare which was approximately twelve miles from Foynes, so it didn't take much persuasion to get us moving. It was partly on our way home – maybe a little bit out of the way. There was also a dance there that night which could go on until the small hours of the morning. Money now was at the end of the trimmings; still with fire in our blood we were raring to go. So having hit the road again we arrived at the carnival late in the evening. It was fairly crowded with every type of amusements and tents erected about the grounds for refreshments with a huge one for the dancing.

Hunger was getting the best of us now. What were we going to do? As I've said money was almost gone and we were a long way from home, especially travelling by bicycle, and with no friend we'd know there to get the loan of a few bob. We wanted to hang on there for a few hours and maybe get to the dance. That wasn't much of a problem as we'd experienced this kind of set-up before. Dancing was in the big tent or the marquee, as we called it. Our plan would be to gain entrance under the canvas but first of all we had to eat. There were six of us all together and pooling our money we discovered that we had enough for two to get to the dance. Tea, bread, and butter and meat were served at two shillings a head and one shilling and sixpence to go into the dance. You took your seats at the table in the refreshment marquee and ordered your grub and when you'd be finished you'd pay the woman that was serving you. Now we had amongst us one hell of a character whom I spent the best of my youth with. He's now passed on to eternal glory. Well, he came up with a plan that we'd order tea for six at a table all to ourselves. Two had the money to pay for it and the plan was when we were near finished eating, this lad would faint and three of us would take him out for air and disappear in the crowd.

As we were nearly finished eating he just leaned over sideways and fell into the lap of one of the other boys. Of course, we played the game. There was great commotion. The woman who was serving us came immediately and got very excited and worried. So we told her we'd take him outside for air and would she get us a glass of water. So she ran off for it and three of us took him outside the door fast. Our other two pals remained as they had the price of the meal. Everyone was asking what happened and one of the lads said, 'Too much to drink!' People were clearing the way for us, having great compassion for the poor sick chap. As soon as we got him out and around the corner of the tent, you wouldn't see us running until we got lost in the crowd, and there was some crowd there at the time.

The other boys remained on, which made it less suspicious. They honestly paid for their meal and made the woman a promise that they'd locate us. But of course that never happened. They did find us for their own convenience but that is as far as it went. Dark was now falling and since lights were not good in those times at carnivals it was easy to get lost in a crowd. While we were taking out our friend who fainted we were in the process of leaving him down when one of the boys spotted a guard approaching us. We whispered to the lad, 'Stay still! There's a guard coming toward us.' So he did and the guard asked us what happened. We told him and he said, 'Take him away out of the crowd and into the air and he'll be all right.' That we did gladly and that was the end of it.

Now for the dance. Two of us had the money to go in and I was one of the two nominated for the job. We paid our one and sixpence and went in in the middle of a very big crowd there. There were seats at the side made of long planks. Before we came in we had selected a spot where the other four lads would linger until we were ready. We'd open the canvas there to let the boys in. We waited for some time until the band struck up and there was a dance in progress. Our job was to open the tyings and I can assure you we had quite a job as the tyings were fairly strong. It took us some time fumbling in the dark with our partners outside waiting and whispering, making sure there was no one around. There were many stewards on the look-out for gate-crashing. We finally made an opening and still sitting on the seat we kept the canvas lifted whilst the boys one by one slid in under the covers. They were seen by some folk inside but that was taken care of with a nod and a wink, and finally all were in and we thoroughly enjoyed ourselves at a great night's dancing. We struck for home about 2.00 am having about eighteen miles to cover over bad roads and we were not as fresh now returning as we were when we started out on Sunday morning. The long hard day had taken its toll on us.

The night was fine and summery with the beautiful fragrance of new-mown hay everywhere. In those times the only tarred roads were the main ones whilst the by-roads which were the ones we were travelling were rough and dusty. But for us they were the handiest as, knowing all that countryside, we took short cuts. It started to get bright after half an hour of travelling and of course the hunger was attacking us again. We came across a few orchards and although apples were not fully ripe it didn't matter to us. We feasted on any rosy ones we came across. If it had been a month later we might have had a feed of turnips as they were very plentiful on the fields by the road.

During the warm summer months, too, farmers would have their milk churns on any running stream available and there were quite a few of them on our return journey. When we came across these it was a real gift. We'd turn the milk out on to the lids and after a good drink of this we were off again like young hares as milk was a great beverage in those times. It was part of our staple diet. There was milk for dinner and supper and always in the summertime we'd drink plenty of it before we went to bed. There was no hay- or cornfield without a big can of it in the shade, maybe under a whitethorn bush with a big square of muslin on top of the can to keep out the flies. I suppose it was that kind of nourishment kept us going and the same with the servant boys. They always had a good drink of milk whenever they got a chance of it and indeed I heard many the hard-working servant boy say that their old boss would try and put some kind of mark on their churns at night to see if they had been disturbed. You daren't turn the churns over as it would leave traces of cream on the sides and that was easy to see in the morning.

The trick was always to have a bit of a twig, give the milk a good stir and disturb the cream which had rested on the top. Then with a cup or a mug or maybe a jam pot you could drink your fill. The lads always had these utensils hidden some place handy for the night. There were many great stories told by the boys about all the tricks used to deter them from drinking the milk. One such concerned the boss who'd be sleeping in the end room and he'd put the milk churns outside his bedroom window so that if any racket were made at the churns he'd be out like a shot. One lad used tell us he'd take off the boots or shoes in a shed nearby and tiptoe to the churns. When he'd be approaching the window he'd go on his fours in case he'd be seen. The lids would be partly pushed on the churns and you'd have to feel around until you'd get a fairly loose one. Of course there'd be the occasional lid would fall to the ground. This could happen while you were foostering in the dark and when this did happen there would be some running and the dog would give tally ho when he'd hear the noise. The boy would make a quick escape and would not return for an hour or more so as to make it look like he wasn't there.

One lad took off the shoes one night, tiptoed to the milk churn, left down his shoes beside the churn, fumbled in the dark at the cover and down it fell, making one hell of a noise. The dogs immediately went wild barking. He ran for his life, leaving the shoes in a hurry. The governor came out with a lighted lamp. The poor devil of a boy was gone helter-skelter and the dogs followed. After a few coaxing words the dogs quietened down, for they knew the lad well, and returned to base. The lad lay low for quite some time watching the boss from a distance and when all was quiet he returned later to collect his shoes. They were gone! When he went to bed in the loft in the outhouse he didn't sleep a wink with worry. How was he going to face the music in the morning? He rose earlier than usual, collected the cows which was his first job, came to the kitchen for his cup of tea, shivering with the thought of how he'd be greeted. The governor came in, the boy went pale and kind of sick but there wasn't a word mentioned. He worked away all day long more determined than ever before. They were at hay all day long himself the boss and a few more lads from neighbouring farms.

Come the evening cows were milked, jobs around the yard finished, supper eaten. He went to his old bunk in the loft to change his old duds to go out for a stroll, to meet the other boys, well-washed and cleaned but with no shoes. He sat on the bed deciding what would he do and reckoned that there was nothing for it but wear his old boots. So after giving them a bit of a cleaning he was up and off. On his way out he had to go through the farmyard past the dwelling-house. The boss came out to tell him he'd be away next day early in the morning and he wanted some extra jobs to be done. Anyway while he was talking to the boy (we'll call him Mick) he'd occasionally glance down at his boots and of course Mick was most attentive. The boss said, 'Will you wait there a few minutes?' In he went to the house, came out, handed Mick his shoes and said, 'Do you know, Mick, some fellow left these shoes by the milk churns last night and went off without them. I was thinking they might fit you.' He turned quickly with an old grin in his face and walked away. The servant boy stayed with that man for many's a year and they got on wonderful together but of course bosses like that were very scarce. Of course there was always the possibility that lads like Mick were very scarce and it was hard to get his equal, as he was an excellent worker.

17

THE EPISODE

After our outing to Foynes we arrived home in good time for the milking in the morning with no sleep – but that was the usual experience after a long journey, having been out all night. I had my thoughts set on the servant boy who had not returned the previous evening to his place of employment. This was considered an awful crime at that time and his boss was a strict hard man with no reprieve whatsoever.

We did our milking at home and I got the pony ready and the milk tanks, and set on my way for the creamery which was about three miles away. Our country road was a narrow one and pretty rough-and-tumble. I had gone about half a mile when out over the ditch came the lad, we'll call him Ned. I was shocked to see him all dressed up in his best Sunday wear and he had hid his bike inside the ditch with his few belongings: working clothes, boots, shirts, etc. all tied up in an old bag attached to the bike. So there and then he informed me he had got the sack. When he returned early in the morning he went directly to the outhouse where he was sleeping and the door was

locked and all his belongings put outside it. So he decided
to wait until the household arose, hoping he could reason
with the boss. He was also owed a few pounds, as he had
settled in January at £45 until Christmas. From week to
week he had drawn a few shillings for fags etc. besides
sending a few pounds home to his mother. There could
be ten or twelve pounds coming to him, which was a great
lot of money at the time. Poor Ned, like all other servant
boys, never kept an account of his money but left it to
the honesty of the boss. When he did confront the boss
he got little sympathy from him. He told him he had
broken his agreement and he had nothing to get. The boss
said, 'All I am giving you is the road.' A bit of a squabble
broke out between them and needless to say poor Ned
felt desperate to be leaving without his bit of money. It
got his dander up and the boss attacked him, knocking
him down on the ground and giving him a good few kicks.

Ned, being young and active, wouldn't stand for this
kind of treatment so he gave the boss as much more as
he took and as he said to me in plain English, 'I kicked
the shit out of him. I picked up my bike and belongings
and left it at that. Only for his wife intervening I'd have
given as much more.' The boss said to Ned as he was
leaving, 'I am going to the garda when I get to the
creamery and I'll get them to follow you.' Ned was
naturally worried as this was the last thing he wanted.
He couldn't face home under these conditions. So he
asked me to keep an eye on him in case he'd report it
because if he did Ned would be honest enough to go to
the garda station and give himself up.

In the meantime he had nothing to eat and I thought

what a raw deal he got to face out on an empty stomach from a house of full and plenty. All I could do was give him his bellyfull of milk by pouring it into one of the churn covers. He drank his fill. I told him to stay in hiding until I'd come back from the creamery.

I proceeded on my journey and when I arrived at the creamery I made contact with a few more servant boys and informed them of Ned's ordeal. They were all wonderful and loyal to each other. As they'd always rally around one of their own when in trouble, I told the boys to keep this in confidence, which they did. First of all they kept our man, the boss, under observation to see if he'd report to the guards. They also gave any little help they could in the line of money to get something to eat for Ned, and I'll always remember one poor chap in particular who hadn't a penny but who was in the habit of getting a bit of tick in a shop. He got twenty cigarettes and gave them to me for Ned. Others gave a few loose Woodbines and one of them got a few empty pint bottles from the back of the pub and filled them with milk to bring back to him.

I must emphasise the fact that in those days when you arrived at the creamery there might be forty or more milk carts in front of you. It might take an hour or so to have your milk delivered and get the skim milk back to take home. We had plenty of time, so, to get organised and find all necessities for poor Ned. In the meantime some of the boys had gone to his boss harmlessly chatting and asking where Ned was that day. The old governor never budged a word except: 'Oh I had other work for him at home today and anyway I had a bit of business to do.' But he never went near the guards. So that was one consolation.

I got all the necessities in the shop: shop bread, butter, plenty of cigs, and went homeward bound on my pony and cart. I kept a close watch so that none of the neighbours would encounter me when I'd arrive at Ned's hideout.

When I did arrive and was just about to tie the pony to a bush, I noticed a horse and trap coming in the distance. I never moved but gave a quick pass to Ned who was just about to come over the fence. I said, 'Stay put! There's a neighbour coming.' He took the bait quickly. The neighbour arrived and pulled up for a chat. I dismissed him with the excuse that I had some rabbit snares set in the field and was going to look at them. Snaring rabbits was a great ploy of ours in those times and a handy way of making a few bob. The neighbour swallowed it, wished me good catching and went on his way. If he had known that I was assisting Ned I'd have been blacklisted.

Anyway with all clear I gave Ned his bit of grub and cigarettes. He tore the bread in pieces and buttered it with a bit of a stick and drank his few bottles of milk. This was done inside the road fence. I also gave him the few bob that was left from the friends' collection. We chatted a little though I didn't delay in case I'd be noticed by any passing neighbour. With his belly full and his poor old heart was full of joy he was happy as Larry.

After a long night without sleep and the hardship he went through at losing his job he said he'd sleep for a few hours as his hiding-place was good and sheltered, and away from the public eye. When I was leaving him I told him I'd be back later in the day with a bit of dinner. That was a chance I could easily get as we had a house full of plenty with always a good supply of bacon as we usually killed two fat pigs at a time; there was plenty of cabbage and praties as well.

So I ate my dinner, which was as usual around one o'clock. When the dinner was finished I'd usually give a hand cleaning the table Surplus praties and their skins were mixed with meal and fed to the hens, of which we had a good flock, maybe seventy or eighty layers. While doing this I was putting away some praties for Ned. Unlike today there would be a big five-gallon pot of boiled praties and also a big pot of cabbage or turnips. My job then was to remove the pots of leftovers to the boiler-house for the pigs. That I did, and I had an old sweet can on the ready. I put some praties and cabbage into it with a good drop of cabbage juice which was a welcome beverage. When I brought back the pots into the kitchen I got a minute's chance to get a skelp of bacon and put in inside my coat. I added that to the sweet can and then gave the excuse that I'd have to go and look at my snares. This was well accepted by my mother and father.

I must talk about the sweet can: all small shops used get these cans full of sweets and when they were empty the shopkeeper would sell them to us for a few pence. They held about a gallon and were very handy on the farm for lots of things such as milk or taking the tea out to the meadow and so on. As a matter of interest my mother used make jelly and custard in the sweet cans as a special treat on a Sunday. As there were twelve of us in family we always required plenty; a little glass bowl or two was no more good than a daisy in a bull's mouth.

Going back to Ned; with my sweet can fairly full I went

back to find him still sound asleep when I arrived. How his eyes lit up when he saw, as he said, the beautiful dinner I brought him! He got stuck into it and ate it all for he had been fairly hungry. He didn't need forks or knives either. I'd have found it hard to bring them to him as they were scarce in our house and if I took any they'd be missed – I'd have had questions to answer.

I stayed for a little while with Ned and as he was anxious to take the cobwebs out of his eyes and freshen himself for the road I went a bit of a distance to a running stream and got him a can full of water. He gave the face a bit of a freshening up and was now ready for anything.

So there and then whilst the road was a bit quiet he said he'd make a start and probably with God's help he'd find some other farmer on the way who might need a servant boy. It was an awkward time of the year in the month of July to get service as all farmers had settled in spring with their workmen and they'd be very cautious and wary about hiring a man at the middle of the season. Of course you'd be bound to meet the odd one. So it was Ned's intention to put a long distance between himself and his past employer. As he said he couldn't return to his father and mother, they'd be disgraced to think he'd lost his job. So we bade each other farewell: '*Go n'éirí an bóthar leat!*' And off he went on his way that glorious summer's day.

I returned home keeping my mind to myself for if my father or mother knew what I was up to I'd never hear the end of it. 'Oh my God!' they'd be saying, 'We are disgraced! What will the neighbours think of us and the son we reared! There wasn't another boy in the parish like you!' They'd be quoting all the good honest farmers' sons and how good they were. This kind of talk was often cast up to me if I was out late at night and God knows I was brainwashed into believing that I was a terrible outlaw. But years after I realised it was all bullshit. And was sorry I hadn't done more for the poor servant boys who had nobody to stand up for them. It was sad to think that a farmer in those times could do a poor hardworking boy out of his bit of money and they had no comeback with no unions to defend them.

As time passed I often wondered what became of Ned and one day at a fair at Charleville – it must have been some years later – who walked up to me but Ned looking great. He told me his plight, how he travelled on about twenty miles from where he left me and went into a country pub, got a medium of Guinness, made enquiries about a job and was directed on to a big farmer who was looking for a boy. There and then he was hired by a very honest farmer. He got good wages and a great house and table and was very grateful to be so lucky so after all his ups and downs. It had a very happy ending and of course he was thankful to me and the friends who had helped him in the time of need.

We kept our silence about Ned and no one, only a few friends, knew what really happened. Our help for him was also kept secret. I often wondered what became of him as that was the last I saw of him. But there is one thing for sure, that Ned and all the other hard-working lads gave a good account of themselves wherever they went.

18

THE JOURNEYMAN SERVANT BOY

The general run of the servant boys and girls came from poor families who lived in cottages and small houses. There were also quite a few very small farmers' sons. The majority of them, however, were strong strapping young men and women. There were also journeymen servant boys or men or, as we'd call them now, dropouts. Many of them were advanced in years, past their forties, and always found it hard to settle down. The causes were drink, broken homes or some other misfortune. They made a very strange type of workman because they were always on the move, excellent whilst they stayed with you but you were never sure of them. They'd be gone when you least expected it or the time they were most needed.

I became, as a very small boy, acquainted with a few of these, as some of them worked for my father and the other farmers around us in the locality. The journeyman would arrive in the early spring or summer or, it may be, autumn - always when times were busy and he would be ready to start work immediately. Of course he'd have been working with other farmers through the country and would move on for some reason or another. He was always very unsettled, his belongings always very few and scanty. He was poorly dressed and badly shod, and looking for any old cast-off clothes or boots.

He was not particular where he slept but it had to be an outside house – somewhere around the farmyard. As I have said in those times there'd be a loft over the dwelling-house, maybe with an entrance from outside by an old stairway or ladder. In rare cases there was a stairs from the kitchen to the loft but this was rarely used by the working lads as they were not welcome to enter the kitchen. In this loft feeding stuff was kept, and potatoes were stored there during the winter for eating until the new ones arrived in June or July. As the journeyman used say, 'It was a great place to sleep as you had great company at night with the little four-legged friends.' Rats were plentiful and it was also a great place for the farm cats to visit. The journeymen's reason for sleeping outside was they always wandered to the pub at night and did not come back until late. They didn't want any of the household observing their appearance when coming home to roost.

Their terms of employment were peculiar. They got their food and bed, and when their day's work was finished they'd get the supper. And on the table would be put a day's wages. Every evening on a plate at the table would lie two and sixpence or three shillings – whatever the arrangements were. So when they'd eaten they'd go out to their rooms in the outhouses where they'd have a mirror with a pan of water and soap. They'd wash and shave. They said that that was one thing they had free and always kept the face clean. They used the old cut-throat razor, as we called it, and with a good razor strap they put up a good edge. It was a simple contraption but it worked. They'd hang the strap up on a nail on the wall or they might shave outside with the strap hanging on a bush. The open razor was rubbed up and down the strap with a quick flick of the wrist and they'd always try it for good edge on a hair on the back of the hand. So with good carbolic soap and a rub of the hands they'd put up a good lather on the face and have a clean-shaven face in a short while. And then it was off for the night . . .

They'd usually drink the most of the money and though it was little, in those days drink was cheap. At that time they might also occasionally buy a bit of tobacco or some fags for they all liked the old smoke. So it was no trouble for these men to walk out from their place of employment as they were never owed any money and as far as they were concerned each day was just another finished chapter with them.

Some great stores were told and were true about these men. One in particular (we'll call him Bill) whom I knew well when I was a wee child used work on this large farm where a few other servant boys were employed. He was a very likeable fellow, as were all the journeymen. Anyway he used tell the rest of the boys at night that the old loft he was sleeping in was full of fleas and he used complain to the missus of the house about this but with no response except: 'Bill, I'll get a powder and kill all them.' So that went on for a while and he was getting fed up with it. One day she said to Bill, 'When you're coming in tonight go to the loft by the outside stairs.' (There was also a stairs leading to the loft from the kitchen which Bill would use most times.) 'I'll be having some friends in tonight and I don't want you coming in through the kitchen.' Of course he wouldn't be too presentable in front of these uppish people. It was OK to have him working on the farm in his usual attire. Then again he might not be too polite after a few drinks.

Bill went off that evening, had his few drinks and, returning before midnight, entered his sleeping quarters from the outside as ordered. The people of the house heard him all right and then everything went quiet. The friends downstairs were being entertained in the best of fashion and with the best of luxuries. There was indeed great commotion and cute Bill had all this under observation from above. After some time he heard them pulling out the table to the middle of the kitchen floor. He left things rest for a while as he had a plan on hand. As he used tell the story he took off all his clothes and lay on the bed, and as he said the little friends in the bed started to attack him so he could stick it no longer. He got up quietly, put one of the blankets around himself and made for the stairs into the kitchen. Strolling down at his ease, with his eyes closed and giving an odd snore and a grunt, he came into view of the boss, the missus of the house and friends. The woman of the house jumped up and shouted, 'Bill, Bill, where are you going?' He stopped in his tracks on the way and surprised-like opened his eyes and looked down at herself and the friends. After a long pause he said, 'Be God, Ma'am, I don't known in the name of the Lord where are they taking me to – maybe the river.' She immediately thought of the fleas and said, 'Bill, please go back up quick and I'll look after them tomorrow.' He used tell that with pride and say, 'Faith, I got a good clean bed next day and whilst I was there for the remainder of the year there wasn't a flea in sight. There was one little drawback: I used be like a mouse coming out of a flour-bag, covered in flea-powder, for she was continuously applying it in case there would ever be a reccurrence of the night of the party.'

Then there was an old bachelor farmer he once worked for. He was well paid but the old boss was very hungry and, as Bill would say, he kept a bad table. So one day for the dinner, meat was rather scarce. Bill got plenty of praties and cabbage but the lump of a big bone he was given had hardly any meat on it. 'Be God,' said Bill, 'the mate is kind of scarce on this bone, sir.'

'Ah well,' the old boss said, 'the nearer the bone the sweeter the mate.'

'For God's sake,' said Bill, 'is that a fact?' Things passed off quietly after the dinner. Bill passed no more remarks but he thought all the more.

Anyway they had a very busy day drawing in hay and forking it into the hayshed. So when evening came to finish the boss said to Bill, 'Unshackle the horse and put him out in the back field.' This was a bit out from the farmyard. Bill did as he was told. So he finished his day, did the milking, got the supper and got himself ready to take a roam out to the pub. Everything passed off well and as usual next morning the boss took the easy job to go out and collect the horse and left Bill to milk the cows. Bill carried on ready for a showdown. The boss returned with the horse and, as Bill said, he was like a bear on a red griddle. He shouts at Bill coming into the yard saying, 'What the hell did you do that for, you bleddy scoundrel?'

'Do what?' said Bill.

The boss said, 'The horse was tied all night to the big stone in the back field.'

'Ah well,' says Bill, 'the nearer the stone the sweeter the grass.' The boss turned away in disgust and of course immediately thought of the big bone he'd given Bill the previous day.

There was another time when he was working on farm where he'd usually give a few weeks every year in the summertime. The woman of the house was very good to him. She used keep a lot of hens running around the farm as did every farmer and she used be chatting to Bill about different breeds of hens. She said one day to Bill, 'I'd love to get a clutch of eggs from Black Minorca hens for hatching.' I must state that Black Minorca were very scarce at that time and they were considered to be great laying hens. 'Do you ever come across any of them?'

'Be God,' says Bill, 'I know of a woman who has a great flock of them. She's living some twenty miles from here and when I am coming next year I'll bring you a clutch of eggs for hatching.'

And she said, 'If you do, I'll pay you well for them.'

Bill finished his season on that farm and then vanished as he'd always do. The woman of the house thought no more of it. Anyway time passed, winter came and went, also the spring. Then summer arrived and never thinking of the past the women got a great surprise when Bill arrived this glorious day in July and to her great shock inside his jacket and shirts he was all skins like an orange.

He had this great lump or clutch of Black Minorca hatch-ing eggs. 'Put them under a hen immediately,' says he. 'I have been keeping them warm for the past week or so and I can tell you they won't take long to hatch out. I have been minding them like a baby, sleeping on my back every night for fear I'd damage any of them. The dacent woman that gave them to me warned me to take care of them as the likes of those eggs were very scarce and she said if anything happened to me clutch of eggs I could never again darken her door.'

The woman he brought the eggs to paid him well when she heard of all the trouble he went through. Bill stayed there working with them and, faith, true to his word the chicks arrived out in less than two weeks, a lovely clutch of Black Minorca, and she was so delighted she slipped Bill a few more bob for all his kindness. And then the poor woman used tell all the neighbours how Bill from the heat of his belly had the eggs half-hatched. In the round-up people were believing that maybe it was easier to hatch egg with a heat of the body than with a hatching hen, if you could manage it. Of course, the rest of the boys when they heard of it used be having good crack, saying to Bill when they'd meet him, 'You're blessed now! No problem getting a job as a hatching hen!' Occasionally at that time people would be looking for a hatching hen or a clocker, and the prime boys would say to them bring in Bill for a few weeks. Knowing the character he was, he'd take it all in good sport.

Anyway time passed on and so did Bill. When autumn came he moved on to another place, putting a distance between himself and the previous employer. One day a good friend of the woman who had the clutch of chickens came to visit her. She was also very good with fowl and kept quite a few herself. She was admiring all the lovely hens and she said to the woman, 'You have lovely Black Minorca like mine. Where did you get them?' So she told the story about Bill. 'Oh my God,' she said, 'the bleady old devil! He was working with us that time and one morning when we got up he was gone. When I went to leave out the hatching hens that evening I discovered the eggs were gone from under one of them. What harm they were down about a week and I was putting the blame on the dogs and every kind of wild animal I could think of. 'To tell you the truth, Bill was the last culprit I thought of.' So putting two and two together they realised that Bill didn't have far to bring the eggs and he didn't need the heat of his body either. So the two women had a good laugh at it all. The woman kept her hens and when Bill came around again it was all forgotten and forgiven. Bill was just another good character and well liked by everybody. As they used say, he was a sweet old rogue.

Seeing that he' drank every penny he earned he was indeed very poorly clad and depended on the generosity of the people he worked for who gave him any old cast-offs they had. One time the local PP, who himself was a generous man, gave him a suit of clothes he had got from some gentleman to give to the poor of his choice. Anyway the PP requested that Bill give up some of his drinking habits so he asked him not to drink on Sundays. And of course Bill being the sweet old rogue he was, agreed; and so for a few Sundays he kept off the bottle. But this got the better of him and one Sunday he broke out. He made his way after last Mass for one of the pubs. He went by the back way so he wouldn't be seen as the PP was always on the look-out for anyone drinking on a Sunday as he was terrible opposed to it.

Anyway the priest got to know Bill was in the pub. He may have seen him himself and, if not, he had a house-keeper, we'll call her Kate, and nothing passed her eye. They used say she had a special stand upstairs by the window with a little hole cut through the curtain and nothing passed her. In those times there were no regular hours for drinking; it lasted till the money ran out. So the PP decided he'd wait up the road and hide until Bill came out and was on his way home. Eventually Bill came along and the PP was not so happy as he was waiting quite a long time. So with two steps forward and one step back Bill was making an attempt to light the pipe when he was coming near where the priest was and of course never expecting he would be waiting for him. All of a sudden the PP stepped out on to the road and started walking towards Bill. From a distance he said in a loud kind of angry voice, 'Drunk again, Bill?' Well, Bill stopped on his tracks and hesitating for a few moments taking the pipe out of his mouth, he answered, 'So am I, Father.' What could the priest say! He had to laugh, for Bill was as witty as they were made and the old roads he'd travelled made him that way.

He was one time employed by a farmer and the woman of the house was very devout. She insisted that Bill would have to join the happy family every night, before going out, to say the rosary which was after the supper:

And there were no steel-bound conventions in that
    old slab dwelling free;
Only this – each night she lined us up to say the
    rosary.

Well of course Bill had no rosary beads and she used
always be promising to get him one next time she'd go
to town. In the meantime a mission came to their local
parish church. This would usually last for two weeks and
there was always plenty of standings outside the church
gate. These were little canvas houses selling all sorts of
holy items, statues, rosary beads and pictures. So, begor,
the missus said to Bill this evening when they were off
to the mission which would usually start at 8.00 pm and
finish at 9.30 approx, 'Here is a half crown for you. Buy
yourself rosary beads.' This was given to Bill as a gift
along with his usual day's wages.

Off he went delighted with his fistful of money and
immediately after the mission he went straight to the pub.
It being the summertime, the missus decided they'd stay
up until Bill would come and all say the rosary together.
As it was mission time they had no chance of saying it
earlier in the evening. Anyway Bill knew they'd be waiting
up for him so he didn't want to show the white feather
and renege after the woman being so kind to him. So on
his way through the farmyard and ready to go into the
house he thought of the beads. He made a beeline for one
of the outhouses and got a bit of a brainwave. He had to
get something to replace the beads. Hanging on the wall
of this outhouse where the harness was kept was a piece
of a dogchain about two feet long, easy to conceal. 'Be

God,' says Bill, 'this will do the trick grand.' In he rambles to the kitchen having a fair share of drink on him with the help of the extra half crown. So the household greeted him and the missus said, 'You're just in time for the rosary.' So Bill got a chair and went to the back of the kitchen behind the rest of the family. Of course with the thought of the dog chain in his pocket he was very protective of himself.

So off they started at the rosary, each member saying their own special decade a bit like the poem, 'The Trimmin's on the Rosary':

> She would portion out the decades to the company
>   at large;
> And when she reached the final one she put poor
>   Bill in charge!

Good enough, he started well, slithering a bit as, of course, he'd dozed off during some of the decades. Anyway he fingered through some of the links of the chain, the Our Father was said and a few Hail Marys. There was a quare noise coming from those rosary beads. She thought for a minute, then looked at the governor who was on his knees beside her, not a very devout man himself. She had a very serious face but he was smirking and so were the family; they knew there was something very odd with Bill's beads. She stopped, quickly turned back towards Bill, still on her knees and said, 'Bill, what part of the decade are you at?' Bill was taken unawares and said, 'Be God, Ma'am, I am just at the swivel.' There was a mighty uproar of laughter from the family and the

158

boss himself whispered across to the missus, 'Remember, porter is sweeter than rosary beads.' Bill as usual was forgiven though she swore she'd stop that half crown the next evening. Of course, she never did and that story was told by herself and him for many a day and there was always a good laugh at it. So the journeyman servants left many a good legacy after them.

19

THE DROLL TYPE

Of the many of these journeymen I knew, there were a few who stood out as men of wit and intelligence and many of their offspring and relations gave an excellent account of themselves all over the world. I knew of one man who was of the working class and this man turned out to be a very successful businessman and became very wealthy.

One of these journeymen, whom we'll call Johnny, was very prominent around our locality, poorly clad and even in the finest weather wearing an old overcoat which was all in tatters. This was discarded when he was working. He also wore a bad old pair of boots and no socks and was always accompanied by a dog, who slept and ate with him every place he went. He wasn't much of a drinker except at weekends but in the middle of his work he might take off and disappear to the pub. He was an excellent worker and any farmer he spent some time with always gave a great account of his services, although the woman of the house would always remark that while Johnnie was around the hens used not lay as well as they did before he came. Whether it was Johnnie or the dog was polishing off some of them they never found out.

He'd work through hail, rain or snow, and I've heard that if in the summertime he got wet, which he often did, out in the hayfield or thinning root crops, when he'd return to the farmyard he'd strip to the skin, hang the old duds on the rope and remain like that for hours until they were dry. He used to say he had great comfort as the woman never ventured out of doors while he was like that. And strange, he used to say the dog passed no remarks nor did the boss for he knew quite well if he did Johnnie was gone like a flash. One time he was hired by what we'd call an eccentric farmer who lived a kind of a hermit's life. He was married and had one son. He kept quiet and reserved and never let his neighbours know what was happening. He'd take his milk to the creamery, get any few messages that were required and kept to himself.

This day one of his cows got sick and as it was the done thing by many a farmer he treated her himself using old types of doses. As time went on she got worse and Johnnie suggested to him to call in the vet but no way! That would cost him £1 and besides he said all the neighbours around would be very inquisitive to know what was wrong. He was not going to bring the vet down his road. At that time the vet travelled by pony and trap as motor cars were a rare thing and if a pony and trap travelled that road, the neighbours would go to the ends of the earth to find out where he was going. They knew in a whip there was a sick animal somewhere. So farmers that time had a kind of a quare feeling about bringing in the vet. It kind of showed that there was a misunderstanding between the farmer and his animals. Anyway the sick cow was kept in the house and got the best of attention day and night. But it was all in vain – finally the poor old cow died.

Now the problem was to bury her without the farmers around him knowing it and so the boss warned poor old Johnnie to keep his mouth shut and needless to say Johnnie did as he was told. The boss said to him, 'I want you to give me a hand tonight when it's dark. We'll dig a hole in the corner of the far field and bury her there.' So come dark, Johnnie and the boss commenced their task. They dug the hole, cutting out the top sod and placing it neatly sideways. Then they pulled out the dead animal with the horse making no noise. Then they put her in the hole and proceeded to cover her with the clay. When they got to ground level the boss got the green top sods and placed them neatly on top, level with the ground so that nobody would suspect there was anything buried there. When this was done everything looked well. But there was one problem: there was a pile of clay left over. The boss looked at Johnnie and said, 'What the hell will we do with that?' Johnnie being so witty said, 'That's no problem. we'll dig another hole and put that into it.'

The boss was not too happy with that answer. He told Johnnie to take the horse into the yard and tackle him on to the butt cart. This he did and came out to where the cow was buried. They loaded up the loose clay on to the cart, dumped in the farmyard and covered it with manure. And as Johnnie used to tell this story he used say, 'I never had such a busy night.' When they were finished it was breaking for day and, as he said, generosity broke out in the old man. 'When we had milked in the morning he told me to take the rest of the day off, and be God I went up into the haybarn and slept my fill.'

Such were some of the old ways of the eccentric farmer and there were many of them at the time. Things like that were what the servant boy had to put up with and keep his mouth shut to keep his job. Johnnie used tell us that this man used say to him when he'd ask why the missus wouldn't do the shopping, 'Sure women all of them are spendthrifts and don't understand money.'

Johnnie had his own peculiar ways too. As previously stated he wasn't a regular drinker; he'd collect up a few shillings and go on a bit of a spree. The boys used say Johnnie would drink every night if he got some fool to pay for it. One morning after the milk was delivered to the creamery he pulled into the pub and tied the donkey to a telegraph pole across the way. He had three churns with skim milk and a bag of yellowmeal for hens and pigs feeding.

So the thirst struck Johnnie. He had quite a few bob saved and like all servant boys he carried his bank with him, wrapped up in a few old rags. In he went to the pub and drink borrowed drink and a few old friends dropped in and so time passed. Naturally the donkey was getting restless and like all donkeys he was a very wise animal. One of what we'd call the prime boys who was passing (we'll call him Sam), noticed the donkey being very uneasy and of course he knew Johnnie was gone on the tear. So he slipped off the winkers off the ass and made it like the ass had pulled them off. He then gave it a tap of a stick and directed him on his road for home. When the donkey got the head free he made off like the hammers of hell and never stopped until he arrived home and into the farmyard. The churns were all disarrayed, and skim milk had spilled when the donkey was rounding a bend. It seems that one of the cartwheels went up on the ditch and the churns turned over. To cap it all the bag of meal was missing. When the boss saw this he was foaming and in a terrible rage and made off with the donkey and cart back the road for the creamery. He located the bag of meal on the side of the road and further on he saw where the milk was spilled.

In a rage he made on for the pub where he knew Johnnie would be and was bent on drawing blood if he got hold of him. But shortly after the ass being let go an old friend dropped into the pub and told Johnnie who did the damage. He knew he had no business going back to his boss. So drunk and all as he was, he made his escape himself – and his dog who accompanied him everywhere. Of course, unlike other servant boys he had no other belongings such as shoes or Sunday clothes, as the journeyman had only what was on his back, and being paid every evening he was owed no money.

Johnnie took the opposite direction to the one where he worked and got a job a few days later at the opposite end of the parish putting a good few miles between himself and his previous employer and he never intended to cross his path again. Time passed by and Johnnie always had it in his head to get his own back some time on the fellow who left off his donkey. Although they were all very loyal to one another Johnnie's old friends didn't like what was done to him.

On Sunday mornings after delivering the milk to the creamery the usual thing for the servant boys was to tie their animals to the poles around the church and go to first Mass so that would give the chance of having good free time until milking in the evening. If they had to wait till second Mass which was at 11 o'clock it would make their day very short for socialising. Considering the way things went in those times you could get a very hefty preacher and you could be there until 12.30. By the time you were home and had the dinner eaten the day was gone. Anyway Johnnie had waited a good few weeks after his ordeal of being left without his ass and as he was about four miles out from the creamery he set off early this Sunday morning on foot to arrive after eight o'clock when the Mass was well started and all animals tied to their usual spot.

He studied things carefully. Always during Mass things were very quiet around the village as most people went to first Mass and those who didn't were still in their beds. So he went direct to Sam's horse and cart, having been well informed that he was at Mass. He took the horse from the cart, left the tackling on him and walked him out of the village on the opposite direction from where Sam worked. After about a mile out he took off the tackling, leaving the winkers on, and left it inside a gate. Then he mounted the horse, rode him for a few further miles and left him off into a field of hay miles from his own place. Not to make things too bad he tied the winkers on the gate so it would give an indication where the horse was. He had the day long to get back to his own quarters. Back in the village it was pandemonium when Sam came out from Mass and discovered his horse gone. And of course the first thing that occurred to him was the day he left the donkey off and the great laugh he had at poor old Johnnie. But of course as the old saying goes: he who laughs last laughs loudest. And it was Johnnie who had won the day. It was never known who took the horse, although all Johnnie's friends had their own idea, and it took days to locate the horse and his tackling.

All these journeymen servants slept rough through the winter, sleeping in old outhouses and haysheds or any place convenient on their roads they trod. They were never worried about a bed or the way they dressed. There was another comical chap, a rare odd individual. He'd also make his appearance in the busy spring or summer but previous to this he'd visit many localities in the winter, not looking for work but just a bit to eat. He was known and well catered for but he had a strange way of eating. He'd get the praties, meat and maybe turnips or cabbage, and he'd usually carry these out in an old can. As his calling was around the dinnertime he'd put his food in the can and go out into the hayshed or maybe cowhouse and there in the quiet where no one was looking he'd feast on what he got from the kitchen. He'd tell the woman of the house that when he'd have this polished off he'd like a bottle of tea to wash down the dinner. This he put with plenty of bread and butter and if he was in a quiet corner he might lie down and have a snooze. After that he'd be on the road again with a 'Thank you, kind woman, and God bless.' Then he'd make on for another house where he'd be sure to strike the supper. On these occasions he'd be usually put up for the night in one of the stables or maybe the hayshed. And he'd usually say I am deadly safe, I don't smoke. The farmer was always sure of nothing happening, such as fire to the hay, and if he offered him a bed he'd rarely refuse it.

Farmers were very glad to see these servant men calling on a winter's night, as they had all the news of the country. They'd sit by the fire until late at night telling all sorts of stories, lies or truth, it didn't matter, as long as they were talking. These men were widely travelled and as one farmer and his wife put it, 'These men are a tonic and as good as any newspaper.' In those bygone days many farmers were not too friendly to each other and one journeyman, called Mick, knew this well. He would shove it on about the man the farmer didn't like with all sorts of yarns, lies and truth. It didn't matter which, for the man he was telling it to was delighted when there was bad news about cattle and pigs dying. As Mick used say the farmer was fattening on all this news. The strange part about all this was that Mick would visit the farmer he was talking about a few days later and he'd skin the other man to him, because he always knew it went down well. They used say that when he'd be telling these fibs he'd close one eye and with the other eye he'd pierce you through to see how this was going down. He'd very quickly gauge how things were going.

One time he called on a certain farmer who was married to a woman from another parish. He knew from information he got in his travels that this farmer hadn't got the full fortune with the woman he married from her brother who was in charge of the home farm. When the father and mother died the son was left in charge of the daughters and was to see they got their required fortune when they were getting married. All their marriages were matches made with a suitable client for, as I must explain, in those days the majority of marriages were the result of matchmaking, especially among the farming class. Love was very little heard of amongst those people. When a lone farmer wanted a woman he'd visit her home and it didn't matter a damn what the girl looked like; the important thing was how much money was in question. Should they come to an arrangement, the marriage was settled for some future date and there was no such a thing as a honeymoon; it was down to work straight away.

Anyway, this farmer Mick was visiting had married the last girl who was left on the home farm and most of the money had run out in getting the other girls wed. Now Mick, knowing this, got a good reception from the farmer and his wife. She too had a bad taste for her brother, who was himself married quite a while and had a big family. Mick set to work telling him how he called to see his brother-in-law some few weeks past and that he was not doing so well. Things were going bad with him and he had to sell a few cows to feed himself and the family. He also reported that when he arrived at the house the brother and the wife were having a hell of a hullabaloo and he had settled things for a while. The man he was telling the story to was in his glory saying, 'Come on, Mick, tell me more and tell me all.'

'Well,' said Mick, 'we had a bit to ate and then I helped him to give the cows a bit of hay, and to tell you the truth it was very bad old hay.' Of course the farmer believed all this and was delighted. When Mick saw the glint in the listener's eyes he was ready to rub it in well. He continued: 'He had turnips and mangolds and they weren't as big as the cork of a champagne bottle.' To add fuel to fire Mick said, 'The oldest daughter, who was about twenty years old, came in. She had been in the town and I noticed she was wearing a big loose old coat and seemed to be rather large. I talked for a while with the father and mother and they knew by me that I had copped something on. The old man himself was like a bear and said to me, "What do you think of our Josie?" I kept my mind to myself as silence is golden. After a while he said, "She's getting married next week," and with a smirk of bitterness, "She's marrying a good-for-nothing servant boy who was working for our neighbouring farmer beside us here." And he finished, "She made her bed and now she can lie on it."'

The man he was telling this to was fattening on all and every bit of this news. What he didn't know was that it was all a pack of lies but it suited. The buck he was telling it to got brainwashed and he'd shout, 'Tell me more, Mick' and indeed Mick didn't leave him short. As he said, 'I wouldn't leave him with a broken heart as the more bad news he heard the better he liked it.' It also helped Mick on his way as he was sure of a few bob when he was going away with, 'The best of luck, Mick. Call again soon and make sure you call to that brother-in-law of mine and tell him the grand place we have and the fine feeding we have for our cows, and make sure you tell him we don't have to sell any cows to feed our family. So I'll be expecting to get a lot more news the next time you call.' But with

Mick that would be many a long day for, after all, those lies and fibs were bound to be found out and would keep Mick barred from that place for a long time. And as he'd say himself, 'I'll have to give them a wide berth for many's the day.'

20

——

THE TIED HOUSE

As well as the ordinary servant boy who worked for his keep and wages there were also the servant men who were married with wives and family (sometimes very big), and these men were given a house on the farm. These would be owned by farmers with maybe a few hundred acres. The house was a poor excuse for a family dwelling, an old iron-covered glorified shed with probably one room and a kitchen, though some of them might have two rooms. I often visited these poor people and you couldn't see your hand in the kitchen with smoke, as these houses always had bad old chimneys. As one poor working man was telling his chums one night about this new dwelling where he was after moving to he said, 'God knows it's great. I have light and water in the house,' meaning that the roof was broken and rain and sunshine came through. Still they reared great families in these old cabins.

Usually these men were excellent with horses and top ploughmen who were eagerly sought by the big farmers. They were also excellent at handling cattle and their ailments. As part of the tied-house agreement they also got free milk, vegetables, potatoes and firewood. They were limited to two or three pints of milk a day which they'd bring home with them every evening. It was collected under the boss's supervision and put into an old sweet can. If the boss was not present he'd help himself to an extra drop and fair play to him for doing this as he'd have a big family to look after. To add to this, the man was usually allowed the grass of a goat, which had to be tethered in case of its wandering on to the farmer's property. Some of these goats were great milkers. Potatoes were not rationed as there was always an ample supply of these grown on the farm, likewise turnips and cabbage. When it was available there might also be a small plot of land attached to the house, where the workmen could sow a few little goodies for the family. In some cases they were allowed to keep a few hens, but only a few. The firewood they got was usually whitethorn bushes which they cut in their spare time on a Sunday or in the evening when there was a bit of light.

If a tree fell by storm on the farm the workmen would be lucky to get some if the boss was a bit generous. He'd make sure he had plenty himself before his men got any. With house-firing, milk and vegetables, they'd get about twenty-five or thirty shillings per week and they worked long hours for this. There were no set times. They might have to work from 5 o'clock in the morning until 8 or 9 o'clock at night, especially in the spring, summer and autumn. Some of these poor men had up to ten or twelve children and it was no joke to bring up a family under these conditions. Getting sleeping space for all them was a serious problem. I remember one poor old fellow who had a house consisting of one room and kitchen. From outside it resembled a beehive. There was an old loft over the bedroom and access to it from the kitchen was by a ladder which would be put outside at the back of the house by day and brought in at night when the children were going to bed. More often than not the ladder would be missing as it was used for many other purposes and, as the children used to tell us, when the ladder was missing they had a special way of going into the loft and they'd put his explanation into rhyme like this:

Shoulder by shoulder
We climbed up to bed
And the last one was pulled up
By the hair of the head.

They'd tell you this with great joy and laughter though living in depressed old times, God love them. They were witty to the end and always made their own fun and enjoyment. These servant men stayed for quite a few years with the same farmers as it wouldn't suit them too much to be moving house with a young family. Their term of employment was from January till the same time the following year. And indeed it was a sad sight to see them on the move with the loan of a horse and cart they'd get from the farmer they'd be moving on to. It would be piled with old pieces of furniture, a bed or two and all kinds of pots and pans, maybe an old bike and always the few hens. It was an awful time for poor people especially in the winter.

They usually made a few runs with the horse and cart

because moving could take a few days. They could be going to a house that might not have been occupied for some time and was bound to be damp and cold. None of them was conveniently placed and the poor woman and children would have to do the moving on foot. No matter how far it was they always had to make their own way. I often wonder how they ever survived – but they did.

Some of these houses were a good bit in from the road. The farmers always liked to have these tied houses somewhere in the middle of the farm where the workman could conveniently keep an eye on the stock. If the workers were lucky and met a generous boss, their agreement could include dinner at the farmer's table with the other servants, a bonus a lot of workmen tried to get in those times. There might be a reduction of a few shillings per week for this which suited the farmer and he had the poor man at his beck and call whenever he wanted him. If he went home for dinner he'd be taking one hour for it as was the agreement but while staying at the farmer's table, especially in busy times, this was often cut short.

When they went home for the dinner the food was not so good. They had plenty of potatoes and turnips but as for meat it was rarely available. The children also met it rough especially if there was a large family for there were no handouts from social services in those times. Yet when I think of it they were far better reared children and more loving than they are today. There was the occasional lucky family who worked for what they called a natural man who allowed them to keep a pig. They'd buy a bonham or two and struggle to fatten them. Then they were in clover as they'd have plenty of bacon by killing the pigs when they were ready. It was the going thing at that time that the poor families who had a pig or two would go around the country houses collecting scraps of leftovers to feed the pigs. When it came to the killing and curing of this bacon crowds of good friends would gather around to help. It was like the wedding of Cana with joy and delight. I was present at a few of these and oh, the excitement that night after the killing! The pan was put on the open fire and pork steaks as fresh as the morning dew were roasted and everyone ate their fill and nothing was wasted. The intestines were cleaned and turned. Then blood of the pig was boiled and mixed with oatmeal and the puddings were filled and made into rings. They were hung on the handle of a brush suspended from chair to chair to season overnight. For a good few days after, all the helpers were sure of a few rings of pudding.

I remember one good old character who had two pigs ready for killing after a tough struggle, feeding with bits of everything he could lay his hands on (and the odd stone of meal the wife would buy whenever she had the few bob to spare). Anyway he was a bit fond of the bottle, as he'd say, never weaned off it from birth. But little he ever had to spend on the family. So when the pigs were ready for killing he was looking in over a half-door at them and the wife said to him, 'I see you are admiring them.'

'I am indeed and do you know, Mary,' he says to her, 'God direct me will I ate them or drink them?' But good luck to her she held the reins and said, 'Faith now, we're going to ate them!' And so they did.

During the busy seasons the wives of the poor men would get a few days' work here and there. There would be *sceallán* to be cut, and making sure that the seed was cut leaving an eye or bud on each piece of potato was a profession in itself. There would be quite a lot of potatoes to get through on some farms, especially when there were three or four acres to be planted, and it paid the farmer better to take on a woman than to put one of his men at the job as the woman was always cheap labour. Women, too, would get a few days at planting and all this brought in the extra few shillings that were sorely needed. There were always shoes and clothes to be bought for the youngsters and there might be one or two of them going for Communion or Confirmation and, of course, they had to be dressed a bit nice for that occasion.

Again in the summer and autumn they would get the odd day here and there. Usually the big farmers' wives would hire one of these women once a week to do the washing of clothes. They used the old washboard and tub of water, and it was rub and squeeze and put out to dry on a line or hedge. It was very severe on the hands but they were prepared for any sort of work. The wintertime was generally a slack time for the women workers as there was not much doing but when it came to December, there were a few shillings to be picked up for Christmas. The local creamery would start buying turkeys for shipping to England and other places at the beginning of December. Lorries would travel to surrounding counties for the purchasing of suitable turkeys for killing. There could be up to a thousand turkeys a day coming to the stores for killing and packing and this is where the poor men and women of the locality picked up the extra few bob. Plucking of the turkeys started around ten in the morning and went on all day and into the night, often not finishing till 1 am.

The women plucked all day long, helped by their children when they came from school, and at night their menfolk would give a hand. A good plucker could handle up to thirty turkeys a day with the occasional stop for the bottle of tea and a few cuts of bread. No *sóannaí* – just plain food. This was brought in by some younger members of the family for there was no such thing as going home for a bit to eat as this would take up too much time. You mustn't forget that the poor people had only two weeks of this bonanza. The price of plucking a turkey at that time was twopence a bird and in the full two weeks a good plucker could earn up to £5, a fortune to the poor people in those times. With the help of some of the family at night they might be capable of creaming off £10 or more, which gave them a wonderful Christmas. The good part of it was they did not get paid until the end of the plucking season so they had all their money in the one lump.

As each turkey was plucked it was presented to one of the creamery employees who gave it a rough inspection looking for flaws such as tears – unless you were a good plucker you could easily tear the flesh. When this quick inspection was done he then gave a ticket to the plucker, who held it until the end of the season. It was enjoyable to watch this carry-on. As each woman got her ticket she put it down into her stocking. The women then wore long black ribbed stockings and by finishing time that night she'd have a fair lump in the stocking. You could always tell a good plucker by the lump in the stocking and the final whip at night. When they were finished they'd move into a corner, take off their stockings and count their takings. Then they'd wrap the tickets up in a piece of paper or cloth and back down they'd go again into the stocking until the pluckers got home, where they'd put them away safely.

I was involved in this process, for as a boy I was employed for the two weeks at the packing end of it. Whenever we were slack at that we were transferred to the plucking quarters. This was a very large long shed with a door at each end. Through one of these the turkeys were brought and this was wired off. All the turkeys for killing were held here until handed out one by one by lads employed for the job. The pluckers would be lined up outside waiting for their prey. There would be four or five gallows and a few 'Pierrepoints' as they used call them (Pierrepoint was the famous British executioner at that time.) Anyway, the killing done, the bird would be plucked as quickly as possible while it was warm as it was easier that way. There would be feathers flying all over the place, which was not surprising when you think that a thousand turkeys were plucked every day.

Some of the pluckers would be a bit on the green side and were bound to tear the flesh. If this was severe they wouldn't get a ticket and if they tore several they'd be banned from plucking. Since this was unavoidable it created a problem. All the pluckers were supplied with seats which were glorified fifty-six-pound butterboxes. Fifty-six pounds was the amount of butter packed into these boxes when they were in use and when they got damaged they were cast aside and so came in handy as seats for the pluckers. Now if the pluckers badly damaged the bird they would slip it into the butterboxes and cover it with feathers. This way they'd avoid being punished. If the tear was, say, a few inches they'd stitch it up again. Every woman carried her supply of needles and white thread so the stitching wouldn't be noticed and a damn good hand they were at this job, as were the men. This was also a bit of a harvest for the boys every night; they'd also turn up for the kill and the extra few shillings and they were also tops at stitching and hiding their damages.

During the night plucking, a large audience from the locality would turn up to watch them as they had no other entertainment and admission was free. They'd pass the night joking and passing cracks about the pluckers. As the plucking finished late in the night all moved for home and all feathers were left there until morning. Then those of us who were employed by the co-op would be posted on to bag the feathers in the morning. They were put into big wool sacks hung from the roof of the store. One of the workers would be inside the sack packing the feathers whilst a few of us outside kept filling. This is where the fun started; as the feathers were collected the torn and damaged turkeys would start appearing. We often picked up to twenty birds from the previous day in one cleaning. You never knew who the culprits were, as it was hard to find out from around about a hundred pluckers. It wasn't a complete loss for the damaged birds were sold to locals at a reduced price. Since it was only the skin that was torn and the flesh perfect, it was a godsend to the poor as they were always sure of a turkey for Christmas got for just a few shillings.

Women with young families would bring their whole clutch with them. They'd sometimes have young ones of two or three years old and they'd be on dummies as we called them that time. (Today we are more refined and call them do-dos.) Anyway these dummies would be put into the child's mouth and from continuous sucking they became crude big yokes. Frequently the dummy would fall out into the feathers and never was seen such commotion looking for the dummies in a pack of feathers. Finally it would be found and with a rub of the apron it was put back into the child's mouth. (Nowadays they would wash it under the tap in case of germs. But, by God, germs didn't exist in those times and all these children grew up to be great men and women.)

As the season came to an end and payday arrived all men and women lined up outside the creamery office to cash in their tickets. After a hard plucking season the long-awaited money was at hand. With bundles of tickets bulging in their pockets or in an old handbag, the pluckers waited until the cash was handed out by some shrewd scrutinising lady or gent making sure there was nothing above or below. The bundle of tickets were taken through a hatch and handed down to a man at a table who counted and recounted every one of them as if they were gold nuggets whilst the client at the hatch taking the tickets viewed the presenter with a very distant look. The money was counted out carefully, pounds, shillings and pence and oh the sheer delight on the faces of the women when they got their handful of money, 'greenbacks', as they called them, which were £1 notes. Maybe an odd women who had a lot of plucking done would get a 'blueback' - a £10 note. All would be gathered gently as if they were eggs and the woman would retreat to some shady corner and with the help of the family make another check on their collection to make sure it was all there. Then it was rolled up carefully and put in a pouch or bag with a bit of string tied around it and maybe put back down the heavy black ribbed stocking where the plucking tickets were kept.

Then off to one of the grocery shops to buy sausages, rashers, black and white pudding, loaf bread and a pot of jam, this maybe the big five-pound pot to have the plenty. They bought confectionery, cake and barmbrack with sweets for the children, a good tossin' (that was a paper rolled and sweets put into it) for each one of them. And then there was the promise of Christmas toys, 'purties' they were called in those times and of course himself if he had helped at the plucking got the price of a few mediums of porter. (There was the odd man that hadn't helped herself and the children and she'd say: 'The devil a fear of him! I don't know if he's worth it!')

One thing was sure and certain: they were going to have a wonderful Christmas and you'd think by the poor things when they'd got that bit of money that they'd never again see a poor day. All these poor people had sons and daughters out in service and they'd also be returning with a little bit of money on Christmas Eve and, God love them, they'd enjoy themselves, happy and united again and living it up for the festival season. They could forget for a while that they would not see that kind of money until the following Christmas with plenty to eat and a good fire as they always bought a few bags of coal for the festive season.

21

—

THE SWEEPER

Among the journeymen servant boys one interesting man
was the one known as the Sweeper, a desperate wanderer
over all the southern counties. He got his name from his
type of work, for he was not a man for the fields or heavy
work although he'd occasionally help at the hay or corn.
And if the woman of the house was busy he was a dab
hand at making the tea and bringing it out to the men or
if any message was wanted from the village in a hurry
such as fags or tobacco, off with the shoes and he'd run
barefooted across the fields to the shop. It was often said
that he was fond of tobacco and since it was sold in
lumps cut off the roll he'd take a few slices from the lump
and it wouldn't be noticed. This was strong cheap tobacco
and strangely he didn't smoke, only chewed it. He was
always with a piece of it in the mouth and chewed it hard.
If anybody vexed him he never spoke but moved up within
a shooting distance. And if you were not prepared you
were bound to get a tobacco spit in the eye would leave
you paralysed for quite a long time.

As his name suggests he was tops at sweeping around

the farmyard and all the farmhouses. He was a kind of a maniac for the brush. He was even known to sweep along the passage leading from the farmhouse to the road which was often a good 600 yards. He seldom used boots or shoes but went barefoot. People used say he had no fear of thorns or briars as he was known to have feet like iron from being continuously barefoot. Likewise he was never known to wear a shirt, only an old pullover in winter time and just his jacket in summer. He used say that shirts were bad for the skin and also a great place for harbouring fleas. As he used to say there was too much heat in the shirt and the fleas always like heat. So that way they'd give you a wide berth. The womenfolk were very fond of him as he was helpful around the house and indeed it was for these types of light jobs he was employed for a very small wage: just a few shillings per week and his meals. He, like the other journeymen, was not particular where he slept. The old hayshed or outhouse would do grand, he used say.

He was an early riser and so as to compensate for not doing hard work he'd have the cows gathered in the morning before the rest of the milkers would arrive and maybe have the horse tackled to the car. While the other farmhands were milking out in the field he'd take the buckets full of milk from them and have ready empty buckets. And he'd take the milk and empty the buckets into the churns or tanks in the field. Because of this the boss looked on him as very handy and it pleased him that the Sweeper was always on the ready to take the milk to the creamery, making the servant boy available for other important work around the farm. He was also fond of a drop taken at the weekend but they used say that if he got it for nothing he'd drink until he fell down.

There was a story told about him going to the creamery one morning and the usual row about whose turn it was to go in. When you'd arrive at the main gate you'd have to study where the other horses, ponies, jennets or asses were. This was so that when it would come to your turn to enter the creamery gap or gate you'd know exactly where you stood so there would be no squabbling. Although there was no morning that went without some fight about whose turn it was.

So this morning the Sweeper as usual studied his opponents and finally he arrived at the gap to go in to deliver his milk. Unfortunately he met Big Jake, a very awkward man with a big Spanish ass and three tanks of milk, who insisted he was there before the Sweeper. But he was wronging him and a little bit of an argument got up between the two of them. As usual there were plenty of prime boys about, egging on the poor old Sweeper and his opposite partner. You'd have some buckos saying to both of them, 'You're in front of him!' The Sweeper knew he was in the right, the onlookers were anxious for a row between them and things were getting hot. The Sweeper just turned his back to the man he was arguing with, slipped a bit of tobacco which was always ready into his mouth and started to chew fairly heavy. He did his best to prolong the argument so as to have the tobacco chewed. In the meantime he was trying to get his horse and cart in the creamery gap and the other buck was trying to get his donkey in as well. As the poor old Sweeper wasn't strong enough for his opponent he was pushed to the ground and rolled over on his back. By this time his dander was fairly up. He got up like a shot and approached big Jake, who was about to bring his big ass in the gap and not knowing about the deadly tobacco spit.

The Sweeper was now within a yard of him and looking him straight in the face. Big Jake was smiling, thinking he was on his way in. A crowd had gathered, some of them knowing the score and waiting for the kill. The Sweeper never lifted a hand as he was now within firing distance and all of a sudden as quickly as chain lightning the big fellow and his ass were both hit right on the eyes like a shot out of a gun. The ass turned around and took off roaring and blind, whilst big Jake went around in circles. It took some time to get the ass under control, as he was gone mad with the pain in the eye. He was bumping into other carts and had to be subdued. In this he was like his master who was also in a bad state and didn't open the eye for quite some time. A shot like that could leave a man or beast paralysed for a good few hours and I can assure you nobody bothered the Sweeper for quite some time afterwards.

He was employed one time in a very large farm where there were other servant boys and a servant girl. It meant that the mistress of the house and the boss were able to take off for town to do some shopping, which of course would take the whole day. As the Sweeper was handy around the house the woman decided that while they were away she'd get him to paint the parlour. Having got all the necessary equipment and paint previously she rigged out the Sweeper and gave him orders to do a good job on the most important room in the house.

She gave special orders to the servant girl to keep out of his way so as he'd get on with the job and have it completed when they'd return home. He took his instructions well and so did the servant girl, obeying orders to the last letter. He started in the morning and worked hard, making sure to cover all the pieces of furniture with cloths and pieces of paper. He was indeed very thorough and neat, in his work if not in his appearance. At dinnertime he made his appearance into the kitchen and put away a good feed which was prepared by the servant girl and when he'd finished his meal he returned again to the parlour and continued for a while at his job. Now in the corner of this parlour there was a big glass cabinet which caught his attention occasionally for in it there was a grand selection of liquor: whiskey, brandy and other spirits as all the well-to-do used keep a fair supply of this for their visiting friends.

The Sweeper, being inquisitive, investigated and decided he'd sample some of the drink. He found he rather liked it and after taking a few swigs he continued working. The craze got the best of him and he'd return from time to time to the glass cabinet just for a nip. In case the servant girl might came down to the parlour he decided to play it safe and lock the door into the kitchen. He continued decorating but after a good few visits to the cabinet he felt a little bit tipsy-turby and thought to himself that the servant girl might be a bit inquisitive and be listening at the locked door, and might hear him at the bottles. He decided to wander further afield and so into the next room with him which was the sleeping quarters of the boss and missus. Here he encountered a fine bed of a kind which he had very seldom seen and decided to bring down the bottle with him and drink in comfort. So sitting down on this grand bed he drank to his heart's content.

Time passed and the servant girl did as she was told, minded her own business. Evening came and the pair returned from their shopping spree. The boss said to the missus he'd untackle the horse from the trap while she with the help of the servant girl gathered all the messages and brought them into the kitchen table. 'Begor,' she said to the girl, 'I'll have a look to see how my decorator is getting on.' So she rushed to open the parlour door and nearly put her head through it, she was moving so fast. To her surprise the door was locked. So she shouted to the Sweeper to open the door but there was no reply. She called in vain and when all failed she went for himself. He came running like a bear on red-hot iron, shouting and banging on the door but again with no response. He didn't want to break down the door and he feared for the worst; so out he went to the window to see if he could get a glimpse of the Sweeper but in those times there were very heavy cross screens on the windows and there was no hope of seeing anything. You could not get in through the windows either, for in all the old big houses there were iron bars on all windows as a protection against intruders.

Indeed it was also said that those bars on the windows were there to keep their daughters from going out at night while the mother and father were asleep, for courting in those times was out of the question and completely banned by the parents – until such time as the children, as they'd call them, were old men and women. Anyway the boss stood at the window thinking and suddenly he remembered the drink and the love the Sweeper had for it. So he came fast for the kitchen and straight for the parlour door and with one strong heave of his shoulders he put the door flying open into the parlour. There was no trace of the Sweeper and in a tear he went straight for the bedroom and there he was snoring in his glory in their bed fully clothed in his rags, half-covered with paint. Although he was tasty at this job he had got a bit careless when the drink got a hold of him and he had done a lot of messing with the paintbrush.

There was one thing that saved him from a good beating and that was his dangerous weapon, the tobacco spit. The boss took him easy and kept his distance, knowing his means of attack. He caught him by the legs and shook him. Immediately the Sweeper awoke, hopped on the floor and instinct struck him that he was in a bit of a corner. So putting his hand in his pocket he applied the lump of tobacco to the mouth and got ready for the strike. Immediately there was a quick exit from the bedroom by the boss, missus and servant girl, who was there as a sightseer. After a while the boss came back to get out the Sweeper, bringing a chair with him for some protection like a lion tamer. He kept his distance and spoke nicely and asked him to leave the bedroom fast. He knew if he got vexed with the Sweeper he had little chance of escaping the strike. Anyway everything worked out all right and he did leave the room quietly.

There was another time he was working in a very large farm as a handy messenger boy around the house, doing the odd jobs here and there. It was the autumn and the harvest was gathered and threshing time was near. He slept in an old outhouse next to which there was a special well-kept kind of outer kitchen where a lot of utensils and flour and baking necessities were kept. There was a big old-time dresser in the corner where old-time ware was kept and on the shelf of it milk and baking requirements were put. The woman of the house kept quite a lot of fowl including a good flock of geese and always during the autumn there would be a good goose killed on Saturday for the Sunday dinner. Now when the Sweeper came in at night he'd always go to the dresser for a slug of milk from one of the jugs. This Saturday, threshing of corn was in progress and of course the Sweeper was a very handy man at the distribution of the porter to the lads and having complete access to the barrel he helped himself rather generously. When the evening work was done he'd got a great taste for it and off he went to the village and drank whatever few shillings he had. He returned home fairly cut and into the outside kitchen and straight for the dresser for his drink of milk. Now what he didn't know was that the missus was after killing a good goose that day. The killing had been done as usual by ripping the neck of the goose and collecting the blood in a big jug as a kind of a delicacy which was fried in the pan next morning. Anyway the woman had put the jug of blood on the dresser beside the jugs of milk.

Well in comes the Sweeper and goes for the jug of milk as he thought and drank his fill. Next morning being Sunday the household rose very early and the boss said to the missus, 'Go out and call the Sweeper. Tell him to collect the cows for milking.' So out she went and into the old house where he was sleeping and up to his old bunk and lo and behold! the Sweeper was lying on his back and blood spattered all over his face and neck. She gave a loud scream and ran like the hammers of hell, shouting. The boss was in a state wanting to know what was wrong. 'Oh,' she says, 'Jesus, Mary and Joseph! the Sweeper is after cutting his throat.' Of course the boss ran for all he was worth into the old Sweeper's sleeping-quarters and there standing beside the bed was the buck, not a care in the world on him. Immediately the boss went to the dresser and, right enough, the jug of blood was gone. The Sweeper was so drunk he didn't know what he was drinking the night before and when the boss told him, 'Be God,' he said, 'it was a grand drink, I feel fresh as a daisy after it.' The woman of the house laughed her fill and talked widely about this for many a day about how the Sweeper was able to stand up and talk after cutting his throat.

These were the ways of the journeymen and all the honest-to-God servant boys and girls in those days of hardship. They worked hard and kept their religion, always finishing the day with a little prayer. This always kept them on the right track. All the *botháin* and the old tin houses are gone and like the closing lines in 'The Trimmin's of the Rosary':

But the years have crowded past us, and the fledg-
    lings all have flown,
And the nest beneath the Sugarloaf no longer is
    their own;

For a hand has written *finis* and the book is closed
    for good –
There's a stately red-tiled mansion where the old
    slab dwelling stood;
There the stranger has her 'evenings' and the
    formal supper's spread,
But I wonder has she 'trimmin's' now or is the
    rosary said?
Ah, those little Irish mothers passing from us one
    by one!
Who will write the noble story of the good that they
    have done?
All their children may be scattered and their
    fortunes windwards hurled,
But the trimmings on the rosary will bless them
    round the world.